PUSHKIN PRESS

"Gems of literary perfection... Such lucid, liquid prose"                    Simon Winchester

"Zweig's accumulated historical and cultural studies remain a body of achievement almost too impressive to take in"                    Clive James

"The perfect stocking-filler"        *Philosophy Football*

STEFAN ZWEIG was born in 1881 in Vienna. Between the two world wars he was an international bestselling author, famed for his gripping novellas, such as *Letter from an Unknown Woman*, his colourful historical biographies of figures such as Mary Stuart and Marie Antoinette, and above all for his vivid historical miniatures, five of which are included in this book. First published in 1927, these miniatures have never been out of print in German, selling more than three million copies, making them Zweig's most popular work. In 1934, with the rise of Nazism, he left Austria. He eventually settled in Brazil, where in 1942 he and his wife were found dead in an apparent double suicide. Much of his work is available from Pushkin Press.

# TRIUMPH
# AND
# DISASTER

—

## FIVE
## HISTORICAL
## MINIATURES

—

### STEFAN
### ZWEIG

*PUSHKIN PRESS*

*LONDON*

Pushkin Press
71–75 Shelton Street,
London WC2H 9JQ

'The Field of Waterloo' and 'The Race to Reach the South Pole' published in German in *Sternstunden der Menschheit*, 1927.

'The Conquest of Byzantium' and 'The Sealed Train' first published in German in *Sternstunden der Menschheit*, 1940 edition.

'Wilson's Failure' first published in English (translated by Eden and Cedar Paul) in 1940, in *The Tide of Fortune: Twelve Historical Miniatures*, and added to later German editions.

This translation first published by Pushkin Press in *Shooting Stars: Ten Historical Miniatures* in 2013

This edition first published in 2016

10 9 8 7 6 5 4 3 2

ISBN 978 1 782272 74 8

Cover design / art direction by Darren Wall
Cover illustration by Stuart Daly
Set in Monotype Dante by Tetragon, London

Printed and bound by CPI Group (UK) Ltd, Croydon CR0 4YY

www.pushkinpress.com

# CONTENTS

# FOREWORD

N O ARTIST is an artist through the entire twenty-four hours of his normal day; he succeeds in producing all that is essential, all that will last, only in a few, rare moments of inspiration. History itself, which we may admire as the greatest writer and actor of all time, is by no means always creative. Even in "God's mysterious workshop", as Goethe reverently calls historical knowledge, a great many indifferent and ordinary incidents happen. As everywhere in life and art, sublime moments that will never be forgotten are few and far between. As a chronicler, history generally does no more than arrange events link by link, indifferently and persistently, fact by fact in a gigantic chain reaching through the millennia, for all tension needs a time of preparation, every incident with any true significance has to develop. Millions of people in a nation are necessary for a single genius to arise, millions of tedious hours must pass before a truly historic shooting star of humanity appears in the sky.

But if artistic geniuses do arise, they will outlast their own time; if such a significant hour in the history of the world occurs, it will decide matters for decades and centuries yet to come. As the electricity of the entire atmosphere is discharged at the tip of a lightning conductor, an immeasurable wealth of events is then crammed together in a small span of time. What usually happens at a leisurely pace, in sequence and due order, is concentrated into a single moment that determines and establishes everything: a single *Yes*, a single *No*, a *Too Soon* or a *Too Late* makes that hour irrevocable for hundreds of generations while deciding the life of a single man or woman, of a nation, even the destiny of all humanity.

Such dramatically compressed and fateful hours, in which a decision outlasting time is made on a single day, in a single hour, often just in a minute, are rare in the life of an individual and rare in the course of history. In this book I am aiming to remember the hours of such shooting stars—I call them that because they outshine the past as brilliantly and steadfastly as stars outshine the night. They come from very different periods of time and very different parts of the world. In none of them have I tried to give a new colour or to intensify the intellectual truth of inner or outer events by means of my own invention. For in those sublime moments when they emerge, fully formed, history needs no helping hand. Where the muse of history is truly a poet and a dramatist, no mortal writer may try to outdo her.

# THE FIELD OF
# WATERLOO

———

## NAPOLEON

———

*18 June 1815*

DESTINY MAKES its urgent way to the mighty and those who do violent deeds. It will be subservient for years on end to a single man—Caesar, Alexander, Napoleon—for it loves those elemental characters that resemble destiny itself, an element that is so hard to comprehend.

Sometimes, however, very seldom at all times, and on a strange whim, it makes its way to some unimportant man. Sometimes—and these are the most astonishing moments in international history—for a split second the strings of fate are pulled by a man who is a complete nonentity. Such people are always more alarmed than gratified by the storm of responsibility that casts them into the heroic drama of the world. Only very rarely does such a man forcefully raise his opportunity aloft, and himself with it. For greatness gives itself to those of little importance only for a second, and if one of them misses his chance it is gone for ever.

## Grouchy

The news is hurled like a cannonball crashing into the dancing, love affairs, intrigues and arguments of the Congress of Vienna: Napoleon, the lion in chains, has broken out of his cage on Elba, and other couriers come galloping up with more news. He has taken Lyons, he has chased the king away, the troops are going over to him with fanatical banners, he is in Paris, in the Tuileries—Leipzig and twenty years of murderous warfare were all in vain. As if seized by a great claw, the ministers who only just now were still carping and quarrelling come together. British, Prussian, Austrian and Russian armies are raised in haste to defeat the usurper of power yet again, and this time finally. The legitimate Europe of emperors and kings was never more united than in this first hour of horror. Wellington moves towards France from the north, a Prussian army under Blücher is coming up beside him to render aid, Schwarzenberg is arming on the Rhine, and as a reserve the Russian regiments are marching slowly and heavily right through Germany.

Napoleon immediately assesses the deadly danger. He knows there is no time to wait for the pack to assemble. He must separate them and attack them separately, the Prussians, the British, the Austrians, before they become a European army and the downfall of his empire. He must hurry, because otherwise the malcontents in his own country will awaken, he must already be the victor before the republicans grow stronger and ally themselves with the royalists, before the double-tongued and incomprehensible Fouché, in league with Talleyrand, his opponent and mirror image, cuts his sinews from behind. He must march against his enemies with vigour, making use of the frenzied enthusiasm of the army. Every day that passes means loss, every hour means danger. In haste, then, he rattles the dice and casts them over Belgium, the bloodiest battlefield of Europe. On 15th June, at three in the morning, the leading troops of the great—and now the only—army of Napoleon cross the border. On the 16th they clash with the Prussian army at Ligny and throw it back. This is the first blow struck by the escaped lion, terrible but not mortal. Stricken, although not annihilated, the Prussian army withdraws towards Brussels.

Napoleon now prepares to strike a second blow, this time against Wellington. He cannot stop to get his breath back, cannot allow himself a breathing space, for every day brings reinforcements to the enemy, and the country behind him, with the restless people of France bled dry, must be roused to enthusiasm by a draught of spirits, the fiery spirits of a victory bulletin. As early as the 17th he is marching with his whole army to the heights of Quatre-Bras, where Wellington, a cold adversary with nerves of steel, has taken up his position. Napoleon's dispositions were never more cautious, his military orders were never clearer than on this day; he considers not only the attack but also his own danger if the stricken but not annihilated army of Blücher should be able to join Wellington's. In order to prevent that, he splits off a part of his own army so that it can chase the Prussian army before it, step by step, and keep it from joining the British.

He gives command of this pursuing army to Marshal Grouchy, an average military officer, brave, upright, decent, reliable, a cavalry commander who has often proved his worth, but only a cavalry commander, no more. Not a hot-headed berserker of a cavalryman like Murat, not a strategist like Saint-Cyr and Berthier, not a hero like Ney. No warlike cuirass adorns his breast, no myth surrounds his figure, no visible quality gives him fame and a position in the heroic world of the Napoleonic legend; he is famous only for his bad luck and misfortune. He has fought in all the battles of the past twenty years, from Spain to Russia, from the Netherlands to Italy, he has slowly risen to the rank of Marshal, which is not undeserved but has been earned for no outstanding deed. The bullets of the Austrians, the sun of Egypt, the daggers of the Arabs, the frost of Russia have cleared his predecessors out of his way—Desaix at Marengo, Kléber in Cairo, Lannes at Wagram—the way to the highest military rank. He has not taken it by storm; twenty years of war have left it open to him.

Napoleon probably knows that in Grouchy he has no hero or strategist, only a reliable, loyal, good and modest man. But half of his marshals are dead and buried, the others, morose, have stayed on their estates, tired of the constant bivouacking. So he is obliged to entrust a crucial mission to a man of moderate talent.

On 17th June, at eleven in the morning, a day after the victory at Ligny, a day before Waterloo, Napoleon gives Marshal Grouchy an independent command for the first time. For a moment, for a single day, the modest Grouchy steps out of the military hierarchy into world history. Only for a moment, but what a moment! Napoleon's orders are clear. While he himself challenges the British, Grouchy is to pursue the Prussians with a third of the army. It looks like a simple mission, straightforward and unmistakable, yet it is also pliable as a double-edged sword. For at the same time as he goes after the Prussians, Grouchy has orders to keep in touch with the main body of the army at all times.

The marshal takes over his command with some hesitation. He is not used to acting independently, his normal preference for circumspection rather than initiative makes him feel secure only when the emperor's brilliant eye tells him what to do. He is also aware of the discontent of the generals behind him, and perhaps he also senses the dark wings of destiny beating. Only the proximity of headquarters is reassuring, for no more than three hours of forced marching separate his army from the imperial troops.

Grouchy takes his leave in pouring rain. His men move slowly after the Prussians, or at least going the way that they think Blücher and his soldiers took, over the spongy, muddy ground.

### The Night in Le Caillou

The northern rain streams down incessantly. Napoleon's regiments trot along in the dark like a herd of wet livestock, every man with two pounds of mud on the soles of his boots; there is no shelter in sight, no house, not so much as a roof. The straw is too soggy for anyone to lie down on it, so groups of ten or twelve soldiers gather close together and sleep sitting upright, back to back, in the torrential rain. The emperor himself does not rest. His nervous febrility keeps him pacing up and down, for the men who go out to reconnoitre find the rain impenetrable, and reports brought back by scouts are at best confused. He still does not know whether Wellington will accept his challenge to give battle, and no news of the Prussians has come from Grouchy yet. So at one in the morning, ignoring the cloudburst as the rain goes on, he is striding along the line of outposts to within firing range of the British bivouacs, which show a faint, smoky light in the mist now and then, and thinking about his plan of attack. Only as day begins to dawn does he return to the little hut in his shabby headquarters at Le Caillou, where he finds Grouchy's first dispatches: confused reports of the retreat of the Prussians, but at least there is the reassuring promise to keep following them. The rain gradually slackens. The emperor paces impatiently up and down his room and stares at the yellow horizon to see whether the terrain in the distance will be revealed at last—and with it his decision.

At five in the morning—the rain has stopped—his inner cloud, a cloud of indecision, also clears. The order is given: the whole army is to form up in rank and file, ready to attack, at nine in the morning. Orderlies gallop off in all directions. Soon drums are beating to summon the men. Only now does Napoleon throw himself on his camp bed to sleep for two hours.

## The Morning of Waterloo

Nine in the morning, but the troops are not yet assembled in their full numbers. The ground underfoot, sodden after three days of rain, makes every movement difficult, and slows down the artillery as the guns come up. The sun appears only slowly, shining in a sharp wind, but it is not the sun of Austerlitz, radiant in a bright sky and promising good fortune; this northerly light is dull and sullen. But at last the troops are ready and now, before the battle begins, Napoleon rides his mare all along the front once more. The eagles on the banners bow down as if in a roaring gale, the cavalry shake their sabres in warlike manner, the infantry raise their bearskin caps on the tips of their bayonets in greeting. All the drums roll, the trumpets sound to greet their field marshal, but above all these sparkling notes, rolling thunderously above the regiments, rises the jubilant cry of *Vive l'empereur!* from the throats of 70,000 soldiers.

No parade in Napoleon's twenty-year reign was more spectacular and enthusiastic than this, the last of them. The cries of acclamation have hardly died away at eleven o'clock—two hours later than foreseen, two fateful hours later!—than the gunners are given the order to mow down the redcoats on the hill with case-shot. Then Ney, "the bravest of the brave", advances with the infantry, and Napoleon's deciding hour begins. The battle has been described a thousand times, but we never tire of reading the exciting accounts of its vicissitudes, whether in Sir Walter Scott's fine version or in Stendhal's episodic rendering. It is seen from both near and far, from the hill where the field marshals met or from the cuirassier's saddle, as a great incident, rich in diversity; it is a work of art with tension and drama brought to bear on its constant alternation of hope and fear, suddenly resolving into a moment of extreme catastrophe. And it is a model of a genuine tragedy, because the fate of Europe was determined in one man's destiny, and the fantastic firework of Napoleon's existence shoots up once more into the skies, before flickering as it falls and goes out.

From eleven to one o'clock, the French regiments storm the heights, take villages and military positions, are thrown back, storm into the attack once more. Ten thousand men already lie dead on the wet, muddy hills of the empty landscape, and nothing has been achieved but the exhaustion of the two adversaries. Both armies are tired to death, both commanders are uneasy. They both know that the victory will go to whichever of them gets reinforcements first, Wellington from Blücher, Napoleon from Grouchy. Napoleon keeps nervously raising his telescope, he keeps sending more orderlies out. If his marshal arrives in time, the sun of Austerlitz will shine over France again.

## Grouchy Loses His Way

Meanwhile Grouchy, unaware that he holds Napoleon's destiny in his hands, has set out according to his orders on the evening of 17th June, following the Prussians in the prescribed direction. The rain has stopped. The young companies who tasted gunpowder for the first time yesterday stroll along, as carefree as in peacetime; the enemy is still not in evidence, there is still no trace of the defeated Prussian army.

Then suddenly, just as the marshal is eating a quick breakfast in a farmhouse, the ground shakes slightly under their feet. They prick up their ears. The sound rolls over the country towards them with a muted tone that is already dying away: they are hearing cannon, batteries of them, being fired far away, but not too far away. A march of three hours, at the most, will get them there. A few of the officers throw themselves down on the ground, in the style of American Indians, to get a clear idea of the direction the sound is coming from. That distant noise is constant and muted. It is the cannonade of Saint-Jean, the beginning of Waterloo. Grouchy holds a council of war. General Gérard, one of the commanders under him, a hot-headed and fiery soldier, wants them to make haste in the direction of the gunfire—"*il faut marcher aux canons*". A second officer agrees: they must get there as fast as they can. None of them is in any doubt that the emperor has attacked the British, and a fierce battle is in progress. Grouchy is not so sure. Used as he is to obeying, he sticks anxiously to his handwritten sheet of paper, the emperor's orders to him to pursue the retreating Prussians. Gérard becomes more insistent when he sees his superior officer's hesitation. "*Marchez aux canons!*" This time he makes it sound like a command, not a suggestion. That displeases Grouchy. He explains, more strongly and sternly, that he cannot deviate from his orders unless word comes from the emperor cancelling them. The officers are disappointed, and the cannon thunder on against the background of a hostile silence.

Gérard tries for the last time: he begs and pleads to be allowed at least to go to the battlefield with his division and some of the cavalry, pledging himself to be on the spot in good time. Grouchy thinks it over. He thinks it over for the length of a second.

## The History of the World in a Moment

Grouchy thinks it over for a second, and that single second shapes his own destiny, Napoleon's, and the destiny of the world. That second in a farmhouse in Walhain decides the course of the whole nineteenth century, and its immortality hangs on the lips of a very brave but very ordinary man, it lies flat and open in his hands as they nervously crumple the emperor's fateful order in his fingers. If Grouchy could pluck up his courage now, if he could be bold enough to disobey that order out of belief in himself and the visible signs he sees, France would be saved. But a natural subaltern will always obey the orders he was given, rather than the call of destiny.

And so Grouchy firmly declines to change their plan. It would be irresponsible, he says, to split up such a small corps even more. His orders are to pursue the Prussians, no more. He declines to act in defiance of the emperor's orders. The officers, in morose mood, say nothing. Silence falls round him. And in that silence the deciding second is gone, and cannot be recalled by words or deeds. Wellington has won. So they march on, Gérard and Vandamme with fists clenched in anger, Grouchy soon feeling ill at ease and less and less sure of himself with every hour that passes—for, strange to say, there is still no sign of the Prussians. They are obviously not on the route going straight to Brussels, and messengers soon report suspicious signs that their retreat has turned into a flanking march to the battlefield. There would still be time to put on a last quick spurt and come to the emperor's aid, and Grouchy waits with increasing impatience for the message bringing an order to go back. But no news comes. Only the muted sound of the cannon thunders over the shaking ground, but from farther and farther away: the guns are casting the iron dice of Waterloo.

## The Afternoon of Waterloo

By now it is one o'clock. It is true that four attacks have been repulsed, but they have done considerable damage to the emperor's centre; Napoleon is already preparing for the crucial storm. He has the batteries in front of La Belle-Alliance reinforced, and before the cannonade lowers its cloudy curtain between the hills, Napoleon casts one last glance over the battlefield.

Looking to the north-east, he sees a dark shadow moving forward as if it were flowing out of the woods: more troops! At once he turns his telescope that way; is it Grouchy who has boldly exceeded his orders and now, miraculously, is arriving at just the right moment? No, says a prisoner who has been brought in, it is the advance guard of General von Blücher's army. Prussian troops are on their way. For the first time, the emperor realizes that the defeated Prussians must have eluded pursuit to join the British early, while a third of his own troops are manoeuvring uselessly in open country. He immediately writes Grouchy a letter telling him at all costs to keep in contact with the Prussians and prevent them from joining the battle.

At the same time Marshal Ney receives the order to attack. Wellington must be repelled before the Prussians arrive. No risk seems too great to take now that the chances are so suddenly reduced. All afternoon ferocious attacks on the plateau go on, and the infantry are always thrown back again. Again they storm the ruined villages, again and again they are smashed to the ground, again and again the wave of infantrymen rises, banners fluttering, to advance on the squares of their adversaries. Wellington still stands firm, and still there is no news of Grouchy. "Where is Grouchy? Where can he be?" murmurs the emperor nervously as he sees the Prussian advance guard gradually gaining ground. The commanding officers under him are also feeling impatient. And, determined to bring the battle to a violent end, Marshal Ney—as recklessly bold as Grouchy is over-thoughtful (three horses have already been shot under him)—stakes everything on throwing the entire French cavalry into action in a single attack. Ten thousand cuirassiers and dragoons attempt that terrible ride of death, smashing through the squares, cutting down the gunners, scattering the rows of men in front. They in turn are repelled again, true, but the force of the British army is failing, the fist holding those hills tightly in its grasp is beginning to slacken. And now, as the decimated French cavalry gives ground, Napoleon's last reserve troops, the Old Guard, move forward heavily, slow of step, to storm the hill whose possession will guarantee the fate of Europe.

## The Moment of Decision

Four hundred cannon have been thundering without a break since morning on both sides. At the front, the cavalcades of horsemen clash with the firing squares, drumsticks come down hard on the drumheads, the whole plain is shaking with the noise. But above the battle, on the two hills, the field marshals are listening to a softer sound above the human storm.

Above the stormy crowds, two watches are ticking quietly like birds' hearts in their hands. Both Napoleon and Wellington keep reaching for their chronometers and counting the hours and minutes that must bring those last, crucial reinforcements to their aid. Wellington knows that Blücher is near, Napoleon is hoping for Grouchy. Neither of them has any other reserves, and whoever brings his troops first has decided the course of the battle. Both commanders are looking through telescopes at the outskirts of the woods, where the Prussian vanguard begins to appear in the form of a light cloud. But are those only a few men skirmishing, or the army itself in flight from Grouchy? The British are putting up their final resistance, but the French troops too are weary. Gasping like two wrestlers, the troops face each other with arms already tired, getting their breath back before they attack one another for the last time. The irrevocable moment of decision has come.

Now, at last, the thunder of cannon is heard on the Prussian flank, with skirmishing and rifle fire from the fusiliers. *"Enfin Grouchy!"* Grouchy at last! Napoleon breathes a sigh of relief. Trusting that his flank is now secure, Napoleon gathers together the last of his men and throws them once more against Wellington's centre, to break the defensive wall outside Brussels and blow open the gateway to Europe.

But the gunfire was only part of a mistaken skirmishing that the approaching Prussians, confused by the uniform of the men they take for enemies, have begun against the Hanoverians. Realizing their mistake, they soon stop firing, and now the massed crowd of them—broad, powerful, unimpeded—pours out of the wood. It is not Grouchy advancing with his troops, but Blücher, and with him Napoleon's undoing. The news spreads fast among the imperial troops, who begin to fall back, still in reasonably good order. Wellington, however, seizes this critical moment. Riding to the edge of the victoriously defended hill, he raises his hat and waves it above his head at the retreating enemy. His own men immediately understand the triumphant gesture. All at once what are left of his troops rise and fling themselves on the enemy, now in disarray. At the same time the Prussian cavalry charge the exhausted and shattered French army. The mortal cry goes up, *"Sauve qui peut!"* Within a few minutes the Grande Armée is nothing but a torrential stream of terrified men in flight, carrying everything along with it, even Napoleon himself. The cavalry, spurring their horses on, make their way into this swiftly retreating stream, easily fishing Napoleon's carriage, the army treasury and all the artillery pieces out of that screaming foam of fear and horror, and only nightfall saves the emperor's life and liberty. But the man who, at midnight, soiled and numb, drops into a chair in a low-built village inn is no emperor now. His empire, his dynasty, his destiny are all over: a small and insignificant man's lack of courage has destroyed what the boldest and most far-sighted of adventurers built up in twenty heroic years.

## Return to Daily Life

As soon as the British attack has struck Napoleon down, a man then almost unknown is speeding in a fast barouche along the road to Brussels and from Brussels to the sea, where a ship is waiting. He sails to London, arriving there before the government's couriers; and, thanks to the news that has not yet broken, he manages to make a fortune on the Stock Exchange. His name is Rothschild, and with this stroke of genius he founds another empire, a family dynasty. Next day England knows about the victory, and in Paris Fouché, always the traitor, knows about the defeat. The bells of victory are pealing in Brussels and Germany.

Next morning only one man still knows nothing about Waterloo, although he was only four hours' march away from that fateful battlefield: the unfortunate Grouchy. Persistently and according to his orders, he has been following the Prussians—but, strange to say, has found them nowhere, which makes him feel uncertain. Meanwhile the cannon sound louder and louder, as if crying out for help. They feel the ground shake, they feel every shot in their hearts. Everyone knows now that this is not skirmishing, that a gigantic battle is in progress, the deciding battle.

Grouchy rides nervously between his officers. They avoid discussing the situation with him; he rejected their advice.

So it is a blessed release when they reach Wavre and finally come upon a single Prussian corps, part of Blücher's rearguard. Grouchy's men storm the

Prussians barring their way. Gérard is ahead of them, as if he were searching for death, driven on by dark forebodings. A bullet cuts him down, and the loudest of those who admonished Grouchy is silent now. At nightfall they storm the village, but they sense that this small victory over the rearguard means nothing now, for suddenly all is silent from over on the battlefield. Alarmingly silent, dreadfully peaceful, a dead and ghastly quiet. And they all feel that the gunfire was better than this nerve-racking uncertainty. The battle must be over, the battle of Waterloo from where Grouchy—too late!—has received Napoleon's note urging him to come to the emperor's aid. It must be over, but who has won? They wait all night, in vain. No message comes from the battlefield. It is as if the Grande Armée had forgotten them and they were empty, pointless figures in impenetrable space. In the morning they strike camp and begin marching again, tired to death and long ago aware that all their marching and manoeuvring has been for nothing.

Then at last, at ten in the morning, an officer from the General Staff comes thundering towards them. They help him down from his horse and fire questions at him. But the officer, his face ravaged by horror, his hair wet at the temples, and trembling with the superhuman effort he has made, only stammers incomprehensible words—words that they do not, cannot, will not understand. They think he must be drunk or deranged when he says there is no emperor any more, no imperial army, France is lost. Gradually, however, they get the whole truth out of him, the devastating account that paralyses them with mortal fear. Grouchy stands there, pale and trembling as he leans on his sword. He knows that his martyrdom is beginning, but he firmly takes all the blame on himself, a thankless task. The hesitant subordinate officer who failed to make that invisible decision at the fateful moment now, face to face with nearby danger, becomes a man again and almost a hero. He immediately assembles all the officers and—with tears of anger and grief in his eyes—makes a short speech in which he both justifies and bewails his hesitation. The officers who still bore him resentment yesterday hear him in silence. Any of them could blame him and boast of having held a better opinion. But none of them dares or wants to do so. They say nothing for a long time, their depth of mourning silences them all.

And it is in that hour, after missing the vital second of decision, that Grouchy shows—but too late now—all his military strength. All his great virtues, circumspection, efficiency, caution and conscientiousness, are obvious now that he trusts himself again and not a written order. Surrounded by superior strength five times greater than his own, he leads his troops back again right through the middle of the enemy—a masterly tactical achievement— without losing a single cannon or a single man, and saves its last army for France and the empire. But when he comes home there is no emperor to thank him, and no enemy against whom he can lead the troops. He has come too late, for ever too late, and even if outwardly his life takes an upward course, if he is confirmed in his rank as a marshal and a peer of France, and he proves his worth manfully in those offices, yet nothing can buy him back that one moment that would have made him the master of destiny, if he had been capable of taking it.

That was the terrible revenge taken by the great moment that seldom descends into the life of ordinary mortals, on a man unjustly called upon to seize it who does not know how to exploit it. All the bourgeois virtues of foresight, obedience, zeal and circumspection are helpless, melted down in the fire of a great and fateful moment of destiny that demands nothing less than genius and shapes it into a lasting likeness. Destiny scornfully rejects the hesitant; another god on earth, with fiery arms it raises only the bold into the heaven of heroes.

# THE RACE TO REACH
# THE SOUTH POLE

## CAPTAIN SCOTT,
## 90 DEGREES LATITUDE

*16 January 1912*

## The Struggle for the Earth

The twentieth century looks down on a world without mysteries. All its countries have been explored, ships have ploughed their way through the most distant seas. Landscapes that only a generation ago still slumbered in blissful anonymity serve the needs of Europe; steamers go as far as the long-sought sources of the Nile. The Victoria Falls, first seen by a European only half a century ago, obediently generate electricity; the Amazon rainforest, that last wilderness, has been cleared; the frontiers of Tibet, the only country that was still virgin territory, have been breached. New drawing by knowledgeable hands now covers the words *Terra incognita* on old maps and globes; in the twentieth century, mankind knows the planet on which it lives. Already the enquiring will is looking for new paths; it must plunge down to the fantastic fauna of the deep sea, or soar up into the endless air. For untrodden paths are to be found only in the skies, and already the steel swallows of aeroplanes shoot up, racing each other, to reach new heights and new distances, now that the earth lies fallow and can reveal no more secrets to human curiosity.

But one final secret preserved the earth's modesty from our gaze into the present century, two tiny parts of its racked and tormented body were still saved from the greed of its own inhabitants: the South Pole and the North Pole, its backbone, two places with almost no character or meaning in themselves, around which its axis has been turning for thousands of years. The earth has protected them, leaving them pure and spotless. It has placed barriers of ice in front of this last mystery, setting eternal winter to guard them against the greedy. Access is forbidden by imperious frost and storms; danger and terror scare away the bold with the menace of death. No human eyes may dwell on this closed sphere, and even the sun takes only a fleeting glance.

Expeditions have followed one another for decades. None has achieved its aim. The body of the boldest of the bold, Andrée, who hoped to fly over the Pole in a balloon and never returned, has rested in the glass coffin of the ice for thirty-three years and has only now been discovered. Every attempt is dashed to pieces on the sheer walls of frost. The earth has hidden her face here for thousands of years, up to our own day, triumphing for the last time over the will of her own creatures. Her modesty, pure and virginal, defies the curiosity of the world.

But the young twentieth century reaches out its hands impatiently. It has forged new weapons in laboratories, found new ways to arm itself against danger, and all resistance only increases its avidity. It wants to know the whole truth, in its very first decade it aims to conquer what all the millennia before could not. The rivalry of nations keeps company with the courage of individuals. They are not competing only to reach the Pole now, but also for the honour of flying the national flag first over newly discovered land: it is a crusade of races and nations against places hallowed by longing. The onslaught is renewed from all quarters of the earth. Mankind waits impatiently, knowing that the prize is the last secret of the place where we live. Peary and Cook prepare to set out from America to conquer the North Pole, while two ships steer southward, one commanded by the Norwegian explorer Amundsen, the other by an Englishman, Captain Scott.

## Scott

Scott, a captain in the British Navy. An average captain, with a record befitting his rank behind him.

He has served to the satisfaction of his superior officers, and later took part in Shackleton's expedition. Nothing in his conduct suggests that he is a hero. His face, reflected by photography, could be that of 1,000 Englishmen, 10,000: cold, energetic, showing no play of muscles, as if frozen hard by interior energy. His eyes are steely grey, his mouth firmly closed. Not a romantic line in it anywhere, not a gleam of humour in a countenance made up of will-power and practical knowledge of the world. His handwriting is any Englishman's handwriting, no shading or flourishes, swift and sure. His style is clear and correct, strikingly factual, yet as unimaginative as a report. Scott writes English as Tacitus writes Latin, as if carving it in unhewn stone. You sense that he is a man who does not dream, fanatically objective, in fact a true blue Englishman in whom even genius takes the crystalline form of a pronounced sense of duty. Men like Scott have featured hundreds of times in British history, conquering India and nameless islands in the East Indian archipelago, colonizing Africa and fighting battles against the whole world, always with the same iron energy, the same collective consciousness and the same cold, reserved expression.

But his will is hard as steel; you can sense that before he takes any action. Scott intends to finish what Shackleton began. He equips an expedition, but his financial means are inadequate. That does not deter him. He sacrifices his own fortune and runs up debts in the certainty of success. His young wife bears him a son, but like another Hector he does not hesitate to leave his Andromache. He soon finds friends and companions; nothing on earth can change his mind now. The strange ship that is to take the expedition to the edge of the Antarctic Ocean is called the *Terra Nova*—strange because it has two kinds of equipment: it is half a Noah's Ark, full of living creatures, and also a modern laboratory with a thousand books and scientific instruments. For they have to take everything that a man needs for his body and mind with them into that empty, uninhabited world. The primitive equipment of primitive people, furs, skins and live animals, make strange partners here for the latest sophisticated modern devices. And the dual nature of the whole enterprise is as fantastic as the ship itself: an adventure, but one as calculated as a business deal, audacity with all the features of caution—endlessly precise and individual calculations against the even more endless whims of chance. They leave England on 1st June 1910. The British Isles are a beautiful sight at that time of year, with lush green meadows and the sun shining, warm and radiant in a cloudless sky. The men feel emotion as the coast vanishes behind them, for they all know that they are saying goodbye to warmth and sunlight for years, some of them perhaps for ever. But the British flag flies above the ship, and they console themselves by thinking that a signal from the world is travelling with them to the only part of the conquered earth that as yet has no master.

## Universitas Antarctica

In January, after a short rest in New Zealand, they land at Cape Evans, on the rim of the eternal ice, and erect a building where they can spend the winter. In Antarctica December and January are the summer months, because only then does the sun shine in a white, metallic sky for a few hours of the day. The walls of their house are made of wood, like those of buildings erected by earlier expeditions, but inside the progress of time is evident. While their predecessors still made do with the dim and stinking light of smouldering fish-oil lamps, tired of their own faces, exhausted by the monotony of the sunless days, these twentieth-century men have the whole world and all its knowledge in abbreviated form inside their four walls. An acetylene lamp gives warm white light, as if by magic cinematography bringing them images of distant places, projections of tropical scenes from milder climates; they have a pianola for music, a gramophone provides the sounds of the human voice, their library contains the wisdom of their time. A typewriter clacks away in one room, another acts as a darkroom where cinematographic and coloured photographs are developed. The expedition's geologist tests stone for its radioactivity, the zoologist discovers new parasites on the penguins they catch, meteorological observations alternate with physical experiments. Every member of the expedition has his allotted work for the months of darkness, and a clever system transforms research in isolation into companionable study. For these thirty men give lectures every evening, hold university courses in the pack ice and the Arctic frost, and they acquire a three-dimensional view of the world in lively conversational exchange. The specialization of research gives up its pride here and promotes understanding in the company of others. In the middle of an elemental, primeval world, alone in a timeless place, thirty men instruct each other in the latest scientific findings of the twentieth century, and in their house they know not only the hour but the second of the world clock. It is touching to read how these serious men enjoy their Christmas tree and their spoof journal *The South*

*Polar Times,* to find how some small incident—a whale surfacing, a pony's fall—becomes a major event, and on the other hand astonishing aspects of the expedition—the glow of the *aurora borealis,* the terrible frost, the vast loneliness—become ordinary daily experiences.

Now and then they venture on small outings. They try out their motor sledges, they learn to ski, they train the dogs. They equip a depot for the great journey, but the days on the calendar pass very slowly until summer (in December), when a ship reaches them through the pack ice with letters from home. Small groups also go on day-long journeys to toughen them up in the worst of the Antarctic winter, they try out their tents and consolidate their experiences. Not everything succeeds, but even the difficulties reinvigorate them. When they return from their expeditions, frozen and tired, they are welcomed back with rejoicing and a warm fire in the hearth, and the comfortable little house at latitude 77 seems to them, after days of deprivation, the most blessed place in the world.

But once such an expedition comes back from the west, and its news silences the house. On their way they have found Amundsen's winter quarters, and now Scott knows that, as well as the frost and danger, he has someone else competing with him for fame as the first to discover the secret of this refractory part of the earth: the Norwegian explorer Amundsen. He measures distances on the maps, and we can imagine his horror from what he wrote when he realized that Amundsen's winter quarters were 110 kilometres closer to the Pole than his own. He is shocked but does not despair. He writes proudly in his diary of his determination to press on for the honour of his country.

The name of Amundsen appears only once in the pages of Scott's diary, and never again. But the reader can feel that, from that day forward, a shadow of anxiety lies over the lonely house in the frozen landscape. And from now on there is not an hour when that name does not torment him, waking and sleeping.

## Setting off for the Pole

A mile from the hut, on the hill where they take observations, they always post alternating guards. An apparatus resembling a cannon has been set up there—a cannon to combat an invisible enemy. Its purpose is to measure the first signs of warmth from the approaching sun. They wait for its appearance for days on end. Reflections already conjure up glowing colour in the morning sky, but the round disc of the sun does not yet rise to the horizon. However, that sky itself, full of the magical light of its proximity, the prelude to reflection, inspires the impatient men. At last the telephone on top of the hill rings, and they are happy to receive the news: the sun has risen, raising its head into the wintry night for an hour, for the first time in months. Its light is very faint, pale and wan, scarcely enough to enliven the icy air; the oscillating waves in the apparatus hardly produce any livelier signals, but the mere sight of the sun is cheering. The expedition is feverishly equipped to make use of the short span of light without delay, the light that means spring, summer and autumn in one, and in what, by our milder standards, would still be the depths of a bitter winter. The motor sledges race ahead. After them come the sledges drawn by Siberian ponies and dogs. The route has been carefully divided up into stages; a depot is set up at the end of every two days' journey to store new clothing and provisions for the return journey, and, most important of all, paraffin—condensed warmth in the endless frost. They move forward together, so as to return gradually in single groups, thus leaving behind the maximum load, the freshest draught animals and the best sledges for the final group, the chosen conquerors of the Pole.

The plan has been thought out in a masterly manner, even foreseeing accidents in detail. And there are indeed accidents. After two days' journey the motor sledges break down and have to be left lying there, useless ballast. The ponies are not as tough as they might have expected either, but in this case organic triumphs over technical equipment: those that have to be shot provide the dogs with welcome, warm nourishment rich in blood to give them new energy.

They set out in separate groups on 1st November 1911. The photographs they took show the strange caravan consisting of first thirty, then twenty, then ten and finally only five men making their way through the white wilderness of a lifeless, primeval world. There is always a man going ahead, muffled up in furs and fabric, a being of wild, barbaric appearance with only his eyes and his beard show-ing. His hand, gloved in fur, holds a pony by the halter as it drags his heavily laden sledge along, and behind him comes another man in the same clothing and with the same attitude, followed by yet another, twenty black dots moving on in a line in that endless, dazzling white. At night they huddle in their tents, erecting ramparts of snow in the direction from which the wind is blowing to protect the ponies, and in the morning the march begins again, monotonous and dreary. They move through the icy air as it drinks human breath for the first time in millennia.

But there is more cause for concern. The weather remains poor: instead of going forty kilometres they can sometimes make only thirty, and every day is precious now they know that someone else is advancing towards the same destination from the other direction. Every small incident here becomes dangerous. A dog has run away, a pony will not eat— all these things are alarming, because values change so terrifyingly in this wilderness. The worth of every living creature here is multiplied by a thousand, is even irreplaceable. Immortality may depend on the four hooves of a single pony, a cloudy sky with a storm coming may prevent something for ever. And the men's own health is beginning to deteriorate: some have snow blindness, others have frostbitten limbs, the ponies are getting wearier all the time, and have to be kept short of food; and finally, just before the Beardmore Glacier, they collapse. The men have to do their sad duty: these brave animals, who have become their friends over two years here in isolation, and accordingly companionship, whom everyone knows by name and who have had affection lavished on them, must be killed. They call this sad place "Shambles Camp" because of the butchery that occurred there. Some members of the expedition split off at this bloodstained place and go back; the others brace themselves to make the last effort, the cruel way over the glacier, that dangerous wall of ice that surrounds the Pole, a wall that only the fire of a passionate human will can destroy.

The distance they march in a day is getting less and less, for the snow here forms a granulated crust, with the result that they have to haul the sledges rather than pull them along. The hard ice cuts the runners, the soft ice rubs the men's feet sore as they walk through its sandy consistency. But they do not give up. On 30th December they have reached 87 degrees latitude, Shackleton's ultimate point. Here the last group must turn back, leaving only five chosen members of the expedition to go on to the Pole. Scott looks at that last group. They dare not protest, but their hearts are heavy to think they must turn back so close to the destination and leave the glory of having seen the Pole first to their companions. But the dice have been cast. Once again they shake hands with each other, making a manly effort to hide their emotion, and then the final group turns. Two small, indeed tiny processions move on, one going south to the unknown, the other going north, homeward bound. Again and again, both groups look back to sense the last presence of living friends. Soon the last figure is out of sight. The five who have been chosen for the final stage of the journey go on into unknown territory: Scott, Bowers, Oates, Wilson and Evans.

## The South Pole

The accounts written by the five become uneasier in those last days; like the blue needle of the compass, they begin to tremble close to the Pole. "It is a big strain as the shadows creep slowly round from our right through ahead to our left!" But now and then hope sparkles more and more brightly. Scott describes the distances covered more and more feelingly. "Only another ninety miles to the Pole, but it's going to be a stiff pull both ways apparently." That is the voice of exhaustion. And two days later: "Only 63 miles from the Pole tonight. We ought to do the trick, but oh! for a better surface!" Then, however, we suddenly hear a new, victorious note. "Only 51 miles to the Pole tonight. If we don't get to it we shall be d—d close." On 14th January hope becomes certainty. "We are less than 40 miles from the Pole. It is a critical time, but we ought to pull through." On 14th January hope becomes cheerfulness in the account. You feel from Scott's heartfelt lines how tense their sinews are, tense with hope, how all their nerves quiver with expectation and impatience. The prize is close, they are already reaching out to the last mystery on earth. One final effort, and they will have reached their goal.

## 16th January

"We started off in high spirits," Scott's diary entry begins. They set out in the morning, earlier than usual, roused from their sleeping bags by impatience to set eyes on the fearful and beautiful mystery as soon as they can. The five men, undeterred, cheerfully march twelve kilometres through the soulless, white wilderness; they cannot miss their destination now, they have almost done a great deed on behalf of mankind. But suddenly one of the companions, Bowers, becomes uneasy. His eye fixes on a small, dark point in the vast snowfield. He dares not put his suspicion into words, but by now the same terrible thought is shaking them all to the core: that signpost could be the work of human hands. They try ingenious means of reassuring themselves. Just as Robinson Crusoe tries in vain to take the strange footprint on the island for his own, they think they must be seeing a crevasse in the ice, or perhaps a reflection. With their nerves on edge they go closer, still trying to pretend to each other, although by now they all know the truth: the Norwegian Amundsen has reached the Pole before them.

Soon the last doubt is destroyed by the undeniable fact of a black flag hoisted on a sledge bearer above the traces of someone else's abandoned campsite—marks left by the runners of sledges, and dogs' paw prints. Amundsen has camped here. Something vast and hard for mankind to grasp has happened: in a molecule of time the South Pole of the earth, uninhabited for millennia, unseen by earthly eyes, has been discovered twice within two weeks. And they are the second discoverers—too late by a single month out of millions of months—the second men to reach the Pole, but coming first means everything to them and coming second nothing. So all their efforts were in vain, all their privations ridiculous, all the hopes of weeks, months, years were absurd. Scott wonders in his diary what it had all been for—for nothing but dreams? "All the day dreams must go; it will be a wearisome return." Tears come to their eyes, and in spite of their exhaustion they cannot sleep that night. Sad and hopeless, they set out like men condemned to death on the last march to the Pole that they had expected to conquer with jubilation. No one tries to console the others; they drag themselves on without a word. On 18th January Captain Scott reaches the Pole with his four companions. Now that the idea of having been the first no longer dazzles him, all he sees, dull-eyed, is the bleakness of the landscape. There is nothing there to be seen, Scott concludes, "very little that is different from the awful monotony of the past days. Great God! this is an awful place!" The only strange thing that they discover is created not by nature but by his rival's human hand: Amundsen's tent with the Norwegian flag fluttering boldly and triumphantly from the rampart that humanity has now stormed. A letter from the conqueror of the Pole waits for the unknown second comer who would tread here after him, asking him to forward it to King Haakon of Norway. Scott takes it upon himself to perform this hardest duty of all, acting as a witness to the world that someone else has done the deed that he longed to be his own.

They sadly put up the British flag, "our poor slighted Union Jack", beside Amundsen's sign of his victory. Then they leave "the goal of our ambition", Scott writes, with prophetic misgivings, "Now for the run home and a desperate struggle. I wonder if we can do it."

## The Collapse

The dangers are ten times worse on the return journey. The compass guided them on the way to the Pole. Now they must also take care not to lose their own trail on the way back, not to lose it once for weeks on end, in case they miss finding the depots where they have stored their food, clothing and the warmth that a few gallons of petroleum mean. So they are uneasy about every step they take when driving snow impedes their vision, for every deviation from the trail will lead to certain death. And their bodies lack the freshness of the first march, when they were still heated by the chemical energies of plentiful food and the warmth of their Antarctic home.

Moreover, the steel spring of their will is slack now. On the outward journey the unearthly hope of representing the curiosity and longing of all mankind kept their energies heroically together, and they acquired superhuman strength through the consciousness of doing something immortal. Now they are fighting for nothing but to save their skins, their physical, mortal existence, for a less than glorious homecoming that perhaps they fear more than they desire.

The notes from those days make terrible reading. The weather gets worse and worse, winter has set in earlier than usual, and the soft snow forms a thick crust under their boots at an angle to the foot so that they stumble, and the frost wears down their weary bodies. There is always a little jubilation when they reach another depot after days of wandering and hesitation, and then a fleeting flame of confidence comes back into what they say. Nothing bears witness more finely to the intellectual heroism of these few men than the way that Wilson, the scientist, goes on making his observations even here, a hair's breadth from death, and adds sixteen kilograms of rare varieties of rock to all the necessary load on his own sledge.

But gradually human courage gives way to the superior power of nature, which here implacably, with the strength hardened by millennia, brings all the powers of cold, frost, snow and wind to bear against the five brave men. Their feet are badly injured now, and their bodies, inadequately warmed by one hot meal a day and weakened by scanty rations, are beginning to fail them. One day the companions are horrified to find that Evans, the strongest of them, is suddenly behaving strangely. He lags behind, keeps complaining of real and imaginary troubles; they are alarmed to conclude from his odd talk that the poor man has lost his mind as the result of a fall or of terrible pain. What are they to do with him? Leave him in this icy wilderness? But on the other hand they must reach the depot without delay, or else—Scott himself hesitates to write what would happen. The unfortunate Evans dies at 12.30 a.m. on 17th February, not a day's march from Shambles Camp where, for the first time, the slaughter of their ponies a month before provides them with a better meal.

The four men march on, but there is a disaster. The next depot brings more bitter disappointment. There is not enough oil there, and that means that they must be sparing with fuel, when warmth is the only real weapon against the cold. In the icy cold and stormy night, waking with a sense of discouragement, they hardly have the strength left to pull felt shoes on over their feet. But they drag themselves on, one of them, Oates, with frostbitten toes. The wind is blowing more sharply than ever, and at the next depot, on 2nd March, there is the cruel disappointment of again finding too little fuel to burn.

Now fear shows through the words they leave. We feel how Scott is attempting to hold back the horror, but again and again a shrill cry of despair disturbs the peace he tries to assume. "We cannot go on like this." Or, "One can only say, 'God help us!' and plod on our weary way." "Tragedy all along the line!" he writes, and wishes for Providence to come to their aid, since none can be expected from men.

However, they drag themselves on and on, without hope, gritting their teeth. Oates is getting worse and worse at keeping up with the others; he is more of a burden than a help to his friends. They have to delay their march at a midday temperature of minus forty-two degrees, and the unhappy man feels and knows that he is bringing death on his companions. They are already preparing for the end. Wilson, the scientist, hands out ten morphium tablets to each of them to hasten their end if necessary. They try one day's march more with their sick companion. Then the unfortunate man himself asks them to leave him behind in his sleeping bag and go on separately. They vigorously refuse, although they all realize that his suggestion would be a relief for them. Oates manages to go a little further on his frostbitten legs to their night quarters. He sleeps with them until next morning. When they wake and look out, there is a blizzard.

Suddenly Oates gets to his feet. "I am just going outside and may be some time," he tells his friends. The others tremble: they all know what that will mean. But no one dares say a word to stop him. No one dares to shake his hand one last time, for they all feel, with respect, that Captain Lawrence

E.G. Oates of the Inniskilling Dragoons is going to his death like a hero.

Three weary, weakened men drag themselves through the endless, icy, iron-hard wilderness, tired and hopeless, with only the dull instinct of self-preservation stiffening their sinews to a stumbling walk. The weather gets worse and worse, a new disappointment mocks them at every depot, there is never enough oil, enough warmth. On 21st March they are only eighteen kilometres away from a depot, but the wind is blowing so murderously that they cannot leave their tent. Every evening they hope for the next morning, so as to reach their destination, for meanwhile their provisions are running out and with them their last hope. Their heating fuel is finished, and the thermometer says forty degrees below zero. Every hope is extinguished; they now have only the choice between starving or freezing to death. The three men struggle against the inevitable end for eight days in a small tent in the middle of the white wilderness world. On 29th March they know that no miracle can save them now. So they decide not to go another step towards their fate, but wait proudly for death as they have suffered every other misfortune. They crawl into their sleeping bags, and not a sigh reaches the outside world to speak of their last suffering.

## *The Dying Man's Letters*

In those moments, facing invisible but now imminent death while the blizzard attacks the thin walls of the tent like a madman, Captain Scott remembers all to whom he is close. Alone in the iciest silence, silence never broken by a human voice, he is heroically aware of his fraternal feelings for his country, for all mankind. In this white wilderness, a mirage of the mind conjures up the image of all who were ever linked to him by love, loyalty and friendship, and he addresses them. Captain Scott writes with freezing fingers, writes letters at the hour of his death to all the living men and women he loves.

They are wonderful letters. In the mighty presence of death all that is small and petty is dismissed; the crystalline air of that empty sky seems to breathe through his words. They are meant for individuals, but speak to all mankind. They are written at a certain time, they speak for eternity.

He writes to his wife, asking her to take good care of his son, the best legacy he can leave her, and above all, he says, "he must guard and you must guard him against indolence. Make him into a strenuous man." Of himself he says—at the end of one of the greatest achievements in the history of the world—"I had to force myself into being strenuous, as you know—had always an inclination to be idle." Even so close to death he does not regret but approves of his own decision to go on the expedition. "What lots and lots I could tell you of this journey. How much better it has been than lounging in too great comfort at home."

And he writes in loyal comradeship to the wife of one of his companions in misfortune, to the mother of another, men who will have died with him when the letters reach home, bearing witness to their heroism. Although he is dying himself, he comforts the bereaved families of the others with his strong, almost superhuman sense of the greatness of the moment and the memorable nature of their deaths.

And he writes to his friends, speaking modestly for himself but with a fine sense of pride for the whole nation, whose worthy son he feels himself to be at this moment. "I may not have proved a great explorer," he admits, "but I think [this diary] will show that the spirit of pluck and the power to endure has not passed out of our race." And death now impels him to tell one friend what manly reserve and his own modesty has kept him from saying all his life. "I never met a man in my life whom I loved and admired more than you, but I never could show you how much your friendship meant to me, for you had much to give and I had nothing."

He writes one last letter, the finest of all, to the British nation, feeling bound to give a reckoning of what he did for the fame of the country on the expedition, blaming only misfortune for its end. He enumerates the various accidents that conspired against him, and in a voice to which the echo of death lends pathos he calls on "our countrymen to see that those who depend upon us are properly cared for".

His last thought is not of his own fate, but of the lives of others. "For God's sake look after our people." The remaining pages are blank.

Captain Scott kept his diary until the last moment, when his fingers were so frozen that the pencil slipped out of them. Only the hope that the pages he had written would be found with his body, as a record of what he had done and of the courage of his countrymen, enabled him to make such a superhuman effort. The last thing he wrote, his frozen fingers shaking, was, "Send this diary to my wife." But then, in cruel certainty, he crossed out the words "my wife", and wrote over them the terrible "my widow".

## The Answer

For weeks their companions had waited in the hut. First confidently, then with some concern, finally with growing uneasiness. Expeditions were sent out twice to help them, but the weather beat them back.

The leaderless men spend all the long winter in the hut, at a loss, with the black shadow of the disaster falling on their hearts. Captain Robert Scott's achievement and his fate are locked in snow and silence during those months. The ice holds him and his last companions sealed in a glass coffin; not until 29th October, in the polar spring, does an expedition set out at least to find the heroes' bodies and the message they left. They reach the tent on 12th November, and find the bodies frozen in their sleeping bags, Scott with a fraternal arm round Wilson even in death. They also find the letters and documents, and dig the tragic heroes a grave. A plain black cross on top of a mound of snow now stands alone in the white world, hiding under it for ever the evidence of a heroic human achievement.

Or no! The expedition's achievements are wonderfully and unexpectedly resurrected, a miracle of our modern technological world. The dead men's friends bring back the records of the expedition on disks and films, the images are developed in a chemical bath, and Scott can be seen again walking with his companions in the polar landscape that only the other explorer, Amundsen, has seen. The news of his words and letters leaps along the electric wire into the astonished world; the king bows his knee in memory of the heroes in a British cathedral. And so what seemed to have been in vain bears fruit again, what appeared to be left undone is applauded as mankind's efforts to reach the unattainable. In a remarkable reversal, greater life comes from a heroic death; downfall arouses the will to rise to infinity. Chance success and easy achievement kindle only ambition, but the heart rises in response to a human being's fight against an invincibly superior power of fate, the greatest of all tragedies, and one that sometimes inspires poets and shapes life a thousand times over.

# THE CONQUEST
# OF BYZANTIUM

———

*29 May 1453*

## The Discovery of Danger

On 5th February 1451, a secret messenger goes to Asia Minor to see the eldest son of Sultan Murad, the twenty-one-year-old Mahomet, bringing him the news that his father is dead. Without exchanging so much as a word with his ministers and advisers the prince, as wily as he is energetic, mounts the best of his horses and whips the magnificent pure-blooded animal the 120 miles to the Bosporus, crossing to the European bank immediately after passing Gallipoli. Only there does he disclose the news of his father's death to his most faithful followers. He swiftly gathers together a select troop of men, bent as he is from the first on putting an end to any other claim to the throne, and leads them to Adrianople, where he is indeed recognized without demur as the master of the Ottoman Empire. His very first action shows Mahomet's fierce determination as a ruler. As a precaution, he disposes of any rivals of his own blood in advance by having his young brother, still a minor, drowned in his bath, and immediately afterwards—once again giving evidence of his forethought and ruthlessness—sends the murderer whom he employed to do the deed to join the murdered boy in death.

In Byzantium, they are horrified to hear that this young and passionate prince Mahomet, who is avid for fame, has succeeded the more thoughtful Murad as Sultan of the Turks. A hundred scouts have told them that the ambitious young man has sworn to get his hands on the former capital of the world, and that in spite of his youth he spends his days and nights in strategic consideration of this, his life's great plan. At the same time, all the reports unanimously agree on the extraordinary military and diplomatic abilities of the new Padishah. Mahomet is both devout and cruel, passionate and malicious, a scholar and a lover of art who reads his Caesar and the biographies of the ancient Romans in Latin, and at the same time a barbarian who sheds blood as freely as water. This man, with his fine, melancholy eyes and sharp nose like a parrot's beak, proves to be a tireless worker, a bold soldier and an unscrupulous diplomat all in one, and those dangerous powers all circle around the same idea: to outdo by far with his own deeds his grandfather Bajazet and his father Murad, who first showed Europe the military superiority of the new Turkish nation. But his initial bid for more power, it is generally known, is felt, will be to take Byzantium, the last remaining jewel in the imperial crown of Constantine and Justinian.

That jewel lies exposed to a fist determined to seize it, well within reach. Today you can easily walk through the Byzantine Empire, those imperial lands of Eastern Rome that once spanned the world, stretching from Persia to the Alps and on to the deserts of Asia, and it will take you only three days, whereas in the past it took many months to travel them; sad to say, nothing is now left of that empire but a head without a body—Constantinople, the city of Constantine, old Byzantium. Furthermore, only a part of that Byzantium still belongs to the emperor, the Basileus, and that is today's city of Istanbul, while Galata has already fallen to the Genoese and all the land beyond the city wall to the Turks. The realm of the last Roman emperor is only the size of a plate, merely a gigantic circular wall surrounding churches, the palace and a tangle of houses, all of them together known as Byzantium. Pitilessly plundered by the crusaders, depopulated by the plague, exhausted by constantly defending itself from nomadic people, torn by national and religious quarrels, the city cannot summon up men or courage to resist, of its own accord, an enemy that has been holding it clasped in its tentacles so long. The purple of the last emperor of Byzantium, Constantine Dragases, is a cloak made of wind, his crown a toy of fate. But for the very reason that it is already surrounded by the Turks, and is sacrosanct to all the lands of the western world because they have jointly shared its culture, to Europe Byzantium is a symbol of its honour. Only if united Christendom protects this last and already crumbling bulwark in the east can Hagia Sophia continue to be a basilica of the faith, the last and at the same time the loveliest cathedral of East Roman Christianity.

Constantine realizes the danger at once. Understandably afraid, for all Mahomet's talk of peace, he sends messenger after messenger to Italy: messengers to the Pope, messengers to Venice, to Genoa, asking for galleys and soldiers to come to his aid. But Rome hesitates, and so does Venice. The old theological rift still yawns between the faith of the east and the faith of the west. The Greek Church hates the Roman Church, and its Patriarch refuses to recognize the Pope as the greatest of God's shepherds. It is true that at two councils, held in Ferrara and Florence some time ago, it was decided that the two Churches should be reunified in view of the Turkish threat, and with that in mind Byzantium should be assured of help against the Turks. But once the danger was no longer so acute, the Greek synods refused to enforce the agreement, and only now that Mahomet has become Sultan does necessity triumph over the obstinacy of the Orthodox Church. At the same time as sending its plea for timely help, Byzantium tells Rome that it will agree to a unified Church. Now galleys are equipped with soldiers and ammunition, and the papal legate sails on one of the ships to conduct a solemn reconciliation between the two western Churches, letting the world know that whoever attacks Byzantium is challenging the united power of Christendom.

## The Mass of Reconciliation

It is a fine spectacle on that December day: the magnificent basilica, whose former glory of marble, mosaic and other precious, shining materials we can hardly imagine in the mosque that it has now become, as it celebrates a great festival of reconciliation. Constantine the Basileus appears with his imperial crown and surrounded by the dignitaries of his realm, to act as the highest witness and guarantor of eternal harmony. The huge cathedral is overcrowded, lit by countless candles; Isidorus, the legate of the Pope in Rome, and the Orthodox patriarch Gregorius celebrate Mass before the altar in brotherly harmony, and for the first time the name of the Pope is once again included in the prayers; for the first time devout song rises simultaneously in Latin and Greek to the vaulted roof of the everlasting cathedral, while the body of St Spiridon is carried in solemn procession by the clergy of the two Churches, now at peace with one another. East and west, the two faiths, seem to be bound for ever, and at last, after years and years of terrible hostility, the idea of Europe, the meaning behind the west, seems to be fulfilled.

But moments of reason and reconciliation are brief and transient in history. Even as voices mingle devoutly in common prayer in the church, outside it in a monastery cell the learned monk Genadios is already denouncing Latin scholars and the betrayal of the true faith; no sooner has reason woven the bond of peace than it is torn in two again by fanaticism, and as little as the Greek clergy think of true submission do Byzantium's friends at the other end of the Mediterranean remember the help they promised. A few galleys, a few hundred soldiers are indeed sent, but then the city is abandoned to its fate.

## The War Begins

Despots preparing for war speak at length of peace before they are fully armed. Mahomet himself, on ascending the throne, received the envoys of Emperor Constantine with the friendliest and most reassuring of words, swearing publicly and solemnly by God and his prophets, by the angels and the Koran, that he will most faithfully observe the treaties with the Basileus. At the same time, however, the wily Sultan is concluding an agreement of mutual neutrality with the Hungarians and the Serbs for a period of three years—within which time he intends to take possession of the city at his leisure. Only then, after Mahomet has promised peace and sworn to keep it for long enough, will he provoke a war by breaking the peace.

So far only the Asian bank of the Bosporus has belonged to the Turks, and ships have been able to pass unhindered from Byzantium through the strait to the Black Sea and the granaries that supply their grain. Now Mahomet cuts off that access (without so much as troubling to find any justification) by ordering a fortress to be built at Rumili Hisari, at the narrowest point of the strait, where the bold Xerxes crossed it in the days of the ancient Persians. Overnight thousands—no, tens of thousands—of labourers go over to the European bank, where fortifications are forbidden by treaty (but what do treaties matter to men of violence?), and to maintain themselves they not only plunder the nearby fields and tear down houses, they also demolish the famous old church of St Michael to get stone for their stronghold; the Sultan in person directs the building work, never resting by day or night, and Byzantium has to watch helplessly as its free access to the Black Sea is cut off, in defiance of law and the treaties. Already the first ships trying to pass the sea that has been free until now come under fire in the middle of peacetime, and after this first successful trial of strength any further pretence is superfluous. In August 1452 Mahomet calls together all his agas and pashas, and openly tells them of his intention to attack and take Byzantium. The announcement is soon followed by the deed itself; heralds are sent out through the whole Turkish Empire, men capable of bearing arms are summoned, and on 5th April 1453 a vast Ottoman army, like a storm tide suddenly rising, surges over the plain of Byzantium to just outside the city walls.

The Sultan, in magnificent robes, rides at the head of his troops to pitch his tent opposite the Lykas Gate. But before he can let the standard of his headquarters fly free in the wind, he orders a prayer mat to be unrolled on the ground. Barefoot, he steps on it, he bows three times, his face to Mecca, his forehead touching the ground, and behind him—a fine spectacle—the many thousands of his army bow in the same direction, offering the same prayer to Allah in the same rhythm, asking him to lend them strength and victory. Only then does the Sultan rise. He is no longer humble, he is challenging once more, the servant of God has become the commander and soldier, and his "tellals" or public criers hurry through the whole camp, announcing to the beating of drums and the blowing of trumpets that "The siege of the city has begun."

## The Walls and the Cannon

Byzantium has only one strength left: its walls. Nothing is left of its once world-embracing past but this legacy of a greater and happier time. The triangle of the city is protected by a triple shield. Lower but still-mighty stone walls divide the two flanks of the city from the Sea of Marmara and the Golden Horn, but the defences known as the Theodosian walls and facing the open land are massive. Constantine, recognizing future danger, had already surrounded Byzantium with blocks of stone, and Justinian had further extended and fortified the walls. However, it was Theodosius who created the real bulwark with a wall seven kilometres long. Today the ivy-clad remains still bear witness to its stony force. Adorned with arrow slits and battlements, further protected by moats, guarded by mighty square towers, in double and triple parallel rows completed and renovated again and again by every emperor over 1,000 years, this majestic wall encircling the city is regarded as the emblem of impregnability of its time. Like the unbridled storm of the barbarian hordes in the past, and the warlike troops of the Turks now in the days of Mahomet, these blocks of dressed stone still mock all the engines of war so far invented; the impact of battering rams is powerless against them, and even shots from the new slings and mortars bounce off the upright wall. No city in Europe is better and more strongly defended than Constantinople by its Theodosian walls.

Mahomet knows those walls and their strength better than anyone. A single idea has occupied his mind for months and years, on night watches and in his dreams: how to take these impregnable defences, how to wreck structures that defy ruin. Drawings are piled high on his desk, showing plans of the enemy fortifications and their extent; he knows every rise in the ground inside and outside the walls, every hollow, every watercourse, and his engineers have thought out every detail with him. But he is disappointed: they all calculate that the Theodosian walls cannot be breached by any artillery yet in use.

Then stronger cannon must be made! Longer, with a greater range and more powerful shots than the art of war yet knows! And other projectiles of harder stone must be devised, heavier, more crushing, more destructive than the cannonballs of the present! A new artillery must be invented to batter those unapproachable walls, there is no other solution, and Mahomet declares himself determined to create this new means of attack at any price.

At any price... such an announcement already arouses, of itself, creative driving forces. And so, soon after the declaration of war, the man regarded as the most ingenious and experienced cannon-founder in the world comes to see the Sultan, Urbas or Orbas, a Hungarian. It is true that he is a Christian, and has already offered his services to Emperor Constantine; but, rightly expecting to get better payment for his art, and bolder opportunities to try it, he says he is ready, if unlimited means are put at his disposal, to cast a cannon for Mahomet larger than any yet seen on earth. The Sultan, to whom, as to anyone possessed by a single idea, no financial price is too high, immediately gives him as many labourers as he wants, and ore is brought to Adrianople in 1,000 carts; for three months the cannon-founder, with endless care, prepares and hardens a clay mould according to secret methods, before the exciting moment when the red-hot metal is poured in. The work succeeds. The huge tube, the greatest ever seen, is struck out of the mould and cooled, but before the first trial shot is fired Mahomet sends criers all over the city to warn pregnant women. When the muzzle, with a lightning flash, spews out the mighty stone ball to a sound like thunder and wrecks the wall that is its target with a single shot, Mahomet immediately orders an entire battery of such guns to be made to the same gigantic proportions.

The first great "stone-throwing engine", as the Greek scribes in alarm called this cannon, had now been successfully built. But there was an even greater problem: how to drag that monster of a metal dragon through the whole of Thrace to the walls of Byzantium? An odyssey unlike any other begins. A whole nation, an entire army, spends two months hauling this rigid, long-necked artefact along. Troops of horsemen in constant patrols thunder ahead of it to protect the precious thing from any accident; behind them, hundreds or maybe thousands of labourers work with carts to remove any unevenness in the path of the immensely heavy gun, which churns up the roads behind it and leaves them in a ruinous state for months. Fifty pairs of oxen are harnessed to the convoy of wagons, and the gigantic metal tube lies on their axles with its load evenly distributed, in the same way as the obelisk was brought from Egypt to Rome in the past. Two hundred men constantly support the gun on right and left as it sways with its own weight, while at the same time fifty carters and carpenters are kept at work without a break to change and oil the wooden rollers under it, to reinforce the supports and to build bridges. All involved understand that this huge caravan can make its way forward through the steppes and the mountains only gradually, step by step, as slowly as the oxen trot. The astonished peasants come out of their villages and cross themselves at the sight of the metal monster being brought, like a god of war escorted by its servants and priests, from one land to another. But soon its metal brothers, cast like the first in an original clay mould, are dragged along after it. Once again, human will-power has made the impossible possible. The round black muzzles of twenty or thirty such monsters are already pointing, gaping wide, at Byzantium; heavy artillery has made its first appearance into the history of war, and a duel begins between the 1,000-year-old walls of the emperors of eastern Rome and the new Sultan's new cannon.

## The Only Hope

Slowly, laboriously, but irresistibly the mammoth cannon crush and grind the walls of Byzantium, their mouths flashing as they bite into it. At first each can fire only six or seven shots a day, but every day the Sultan brings up more of them, and with each hit another breach, accompanied by clouds of dust and rubble, is made in the stonework. It is true that by night the besieged citizens mend the gaps with increasingly makeshift wooden palisades and stop them up with bales of linen, but they are now not fighting behind the old impregnable walls, which had been hard as iron, and the 8,000 within those walls think with dread of the crucial hour when Mahomet's 150,000 men will mount their final attack on the already impaired fortifications. It is time, high time, for Europe and Christendom to remember their promise. Throngs of women with their children are on their knees all day in front of the shrines full of relics in the churches, soldiers are on the look-out from the watchtowers day and night to see whether the promised papal and Venetian reinforcement fleet will appear at last in the Sea of Marmara, swarming now with Turkish ships.

Finally, at three in the morning on 20th April, a signal flare goes up. Sails have been sighted in the distance—not the mighty Christian fleet that Byzantium had dreamt of, but all the same three large Genoese vessels are coming up slowly with the wind behind them. They are followed by a fourth, smaller, Byzantine grain ship that the three larger vessels have placed in their midst for protection. At once the whole of Constantinople gathers enthusiastically by the ramparts on the banks of the Bosporus to greet these reinforcements. But at the same time Mahomet flings himself on his horse and gallops as fast as he can from his crimson tent down to the harbour, where the Turkish fleet lies at anchor, and gives orders for the ships to be prevented at any cost from running into the Golden Horn, the harbour of Byzantium.

The Turkish fleet numbers 150 ships, although they are smaller vessels, and at once thousands of oars dip splashing into the sea. With grappling hooks, flamethrowers and sling-stones those 150 caravels work their way towards the four galleons, but the four mighty ships, driven on fast by the wind, overtake and pass the Turkish boats spitting out missiles and shouting at the enemy. Majestically, with round sails swelling broadly and ignoring their attackers, the four steer towards the safe harbour of the Golden Horn, where the famous chain stretched across it from Stamboul to Galata is supposed to offer long-term protection against attack. The four galleons are very close to their destination now; the thousands on the walls can make out every individual face, men and women are already throwing themselves on their knees to thank God for this glorious deliverance, the chain in the harbour falls with a clatter to let the reinforcement ships in.

Then, all of a sudden, a terrible thing happens. The wind suddenly drops, and as if held by a magnet the four sailing ships are suddenly becalmed in the middle of the sea, only a stone's throw from the safety of the harbour. The entire fleet of enemy boats, their crews shouting jubilantly, fling themselves at the four crippled ships standing motionless in the water like four towers. The smaller vessels attach themselves with grappling hooks to the flanks of the large galleons, like hounds attacking a sixteen-tine deer, striking the wood of their hulls with axes to sink them, sending more and more men to climb the anchor chains, flinging torches and firebrands at the sails to set them alight. The captain of the Turkish armada drives his own flagship with determination against the transport ship of grain to ram it. Already the two ships are locked together. The Genoese sailors, higher up than the Turkish boats and protected by armoured foredecks, can fend off the climbing attackers at first, driving them away with axes and stones and Greek fire. But soon the fight must end; there are too many against too few. The Genoese ships are lost.

It is a dreadful spectacle for the thousands on the walls. As close as they are to the bloodthirsty fighting in the hippodrome, where they go for their own pleasure, they are now painfully close to a naval battle that they can watch with the naked eye and see the apparently inevitable downfall of their own ships. Two more hours at the most, and the four ships will be defeated by the enemy pack in the arena of the sea. Their helpers have come in vain, it was all for nothing! The despairing Greeks on the walls of Constantinople, only a stone's throw from their brothers, stand shouting, their fists clenched in helpless rage, unable to help their saviours. Many try to spur on their fighting friends with wild gestures. Others, hands raised to heaven, call on Christ and the Archangel Michael and all the saints of their churches and cloisters who have kept Byzantium safe for so many centuries, begging them to work a miracle. But the Turks on the opposite bank of Galata are themselves watching and shouting and praying just as fervently for their own people to be victorious: the sea has become a stage, the naval battle a gladiatorial contest. The Sultan himself has come up at the gallop. Surrounded by his pashas, he rides so far into the water that his coat is wet; and, shouting through his cupped hands as if to magnify his voice, he angrily orders his men to capture the Christian ships at all costs. Again and again, as a galley is driven back, he rages and threatens his admiral with his curved sword. "If you do not win this battle then don't come back alive."

The four Christian ships are still holding out. But the battle is approaching its end, the slingshots with which they are driving off the Turkish ships are running out, the sailors are tiring after hours of battle against an enemy who outnumbers them fifty times over. The day is nearly over, the sun is sinking to the horizon. Another hour, and the ships, even if the Turks have not captured them with grappling hooks by then, will be carried defenceless by the current to the bank beyond Galata, which is in Turkish hands. They are lost, lost, lost.

Then something happens that appears to the despairing, weeping, lamenting throng from Byzantium like a miracle. Suddenly a slight sound is heard, suddenly the wind is rising. And the slack sails of the four ships at once fill out, large and round. The wind that the Christians have longed and prayed for has reawakened. The bows of the galleons rise triumphantly, with a swelling thrust they overtake and outstrip their pursuers. They are free, they are safe. The first, then the second, the third, the fourth now run into the safety of the harbour to the roars of jubilation of thousands on the walls, the chain that has been lowered rises again, clinking, and behind them, scattered on the sea, the pack of smaller Turkish vessels is left powerless. Once again, the joy of hope hovers like a crimson cloud over the gloomy and desperate city.

### The Fleet Crosses the Mountain

The exuberant delight of the besieged citizens lasts for a night, and night always beguiles the senses with fantasy, confusing hope with the sweet poison of dreams. For the length of that night the besieged believe that they are secure and safe. For as those four ships have landed soldiers and provisions without mishap, more will come now, week after week, or so they dream. Europe has not forgotten them, and already, in their over-hasty expectations, they think of the siege as lifted, the enemy discouraged and conquered.

But Mahomet too is a dreamer, if a dreamer of that other and much rarer kind, one who knows how to transform dreams into reality. And even as the Genoese, in their delusions, think that they and their galleons are safe in the harbour of the Golden Horn, he is drafting a plan of such fantastic audacity that in all honesty it can be set beside the boldest deeds of Hannibal and Napoleon in the history of warfare. Byzantium lies before him like a golden fruit, but he cannot pluck it. The main reason is the Golden Horn, that inlet of the sea cutting deep into the land, a long bay that secures one flank of Constantinople. To penetrate that bay is in practice impossible, for the Genoese city of Galata, to which Mahomet has pledged neutrality, lies at the entrance, and from there the chain is stretched across to the enemy city. So his fleet cannot get into the bay by thrusting forward, and the Christian fleet could be attacked only from the inner basin, where Genoese territory ends. But how can he get a fleet into that inner bay? One could be built, but that would take months and months, and the Sultan is too impatient to wait so long.

It was then that Mahomet made the brilliant plan of transporting his fleet from the outer sea, where it is useless to him, across the tongue of land and into the inner harbour of the Golden Horn. The breathtakingly bold idea of crossing a mountainous strip of land with hundreds of ships looks at first sight so absurd and impracticable that the Byzantines and the Genoese of Galata take as little account of it in their strategic calculations as the Romans before them and the Austrians after them did of the swift crossing of the Alps by Hannibal and Napoleon. All worldly experience tells us that ships can travel only by water, and a fleet of them can never cross a mountain. But it is always the true sign of a daemonic will that it can turn the impossible into reality, and in warfare military genius scorns the rules of war, and at a given moment turns to creative improvisation rather than the old tried and trusted methods. A vast operation begins, one almost without an equal in the annals of history. In secrecy, Mahomet has countless wooden rollers brought and fixed to sleighs by carpenters. The ships are drawn up out of the sea and fixed to the sleighs as if on a movable dry dock. At the same time thousands of labourers are at work levelling out the narrow mule-track going up the hill of Pera and then down again, to make it as even as possible for traffic. To conceal from the enemy the sudden presence of so many workmen, the Sultan has a terrifying cannonade of mortars opened up over the neutral city of Galata every day and night; it is pointless in itself, and its only purpose is to distract attention and cover the movement of ships over the mountains and valleys from one body of water to another. While the enemy is occupied, suspecting no attack except from the land, the countless round wooden rollers, well treated with oil and grease, begin to move, and now ship after ship is hauled over the mountain on those rollers, drawn in its sleigh-like runners by countless pairs of oxen and with the help of the sailors pushing from behind. As soon as night hides the sight, this miraculous journey begins. Silent as all that is great, well thought out as all that is clever, the miracle of miracles is performed: an entire fleet crosses the mountain.

The crucial element in all great military operations is always the moment of surprise. And here Mahomet's particular genius proves its worth magnificently. No one has any idea what he plans—"if a hair in my beard knew my thoughts I would pluck it out," that brilliantly wily man once said of himself—and in perfect order, while the cannon ostentatiously thunder against the walls, his commands are carried out. Seventy ships are moved over mountain and valley, through vineyards and fields and woods, from one sea to another on that single night of 22nd April. Next morning the citizens of Byzantium think they are dreaming: an enemy fleet brought here as if by a ghostly hand, sailing with pennants hoisted and fully manned, in the heart of their supposedly unapproachable bay. They are still rubbing their eyes, at a loss to imagine how this miracle was worked, when fanfares and cymbals and drums are already playing jubilant music right under the wall of their flank, hitherto protected by the harbour. As a result of this brilliant coup, the whole Golden Horn except for the neutral space occupied by Galata, where the Christian fleet is boxed in, belongs to the Sultan and his army. Unobstructed, he can now lead his troops over a pontoon bridge against the weaker wall. The weaker flank of the city is thus under threat, and the ranks of the defenders, sparse enough anyway, have to stretch over yet more space. An iron fist has closed more and more tightly round the victim's throat.

## Europe, Help!

The besieged are no longer under any illusions. They know that if they are also attacked in the flank that has been torn open, they will not be able to put up resistance for long behind their battered walls, 8,000 of them against 150,000, unless help comes very quickly. But did not the Signoria of Venice solemnly agree to send ships? Can the Pope remain indifferent when Hagia Sophia, the most magnificent church in the west, is in danger of becoming a mosque of the unbelievers? Does Europe, caught in strife and divided a hundred times over by unworthy jealousy, still not understand the danger to western culture? Perhaps—so the besieged say, consoling themselves—the fleet coming to their aid has been ready for a long time, and hesitates to set sail only because it does not know their predicament, and it would be enough if someone made the Europeans aware of the monstrous responsibility of this fatal delay?

But how can information be sent to the Venetian fleet? Turkish ships are scattered all over the Sea of Marmara; to break out from Byzantium with the whole fleet would be to deliver it up to destruction, also weakening the defence of the city, where every single man counts, by withdrawing a few hundred soldiers. They decide to venture only a very small ship with a tiny crew. Twelve men in all—if there were any justice in history, their names would be as well known as those of the Argonauts for such an act of heroism, but not a single name has come down to us. An enemy flag is hoisted on the little brigantine. The twelve men clothe themselves in the Turkish fashion, with turbans or tarbooshes on their heads, so as not to arouse attention. On 3rd May the chain closing off the harbour is let down without a sound, and with a muted beat of oars the bold boat glides out under cover of darkness. Lo and behold, a miracle... unrecognized, the tiny vessel passes through the Dardanelles and into the Aegean Sea. It is the very extent of the crew's audacity that cripples the enemy. Mahomet has thought of everything but this unimaginable turn of events—that a single ship with twelve heroes aboard would dare such an Argo-like voyage through his own fleet.

But the disappointment is tragic: no Venetian sails appear on the Aegean. No fleet is ready to come to Byzantium. Venice and the Pope, everyone has forgotten the city; absorbed in parish-pump politics, they are all neglecting their honour and their oath. These tragic moments in history are repeated again and again: where the highest concentration of all united forces should be brought together to protect European culture, the princes and their states cannot abandon their petty rivalries even for a short span of time. To Genoa it is more important to outshine Venice, and Venice in turn feels the same about Genoa, rather than uniting against the common enemy for a few hours. The sea is empty. The brave crew desperately row their nutshell of a boat from island to island. But the harbours everywhere are occupied by enemies, and no friendly ship will venture into the war-torn area any more.

Now what is to be done? Several of the twelve, not surprisingly, have lost heart. Why take the dangerous route back to Constantinople? They cannot bring the city any hope. Perhaps it has already fallen; in any case, if they go back, either prison or death awaits them. However—and all credit to those heroes whose names go unknown!—the majority decide in favour of returning. They have been sent to deliver a message, and they must go home to report on the outcome, depressing as it is. So the little ship ventures on the way back through the Dardanelles alone, and then through the Sea of Marmara and the enemy fleet. On 23rd May, twenty days after setting out—by now in Constantinople all hope of seeing their ship again has been lost, and no one expects a message or their return—on 23rd May a few men on watch on the walls wave their banners, for a small ship, oars beating fast, is approaching the Golden Horn, and when the Turks, alerted by thunderous cries of joy from the besieged city, see in astonishment that this brigantine, boldly passing through their waters under a Turkish flag, is an enemy vessel they come up on all sides to intercept it just before it reaches the protection of the harbour. For a moment Byzantium, uttering cries of jubilation, still lives in the happy hope that Europe has remembered them, and this ship is sent ahead as a messenger. Only in the evening is the truth known: the news is bad. Christendom has forgotten Byzantium. The besieged citizens are alone, and if they cannot save themselves they are lost.

## The Night of the Storm

After six weeks of almost daily fighting, the Sultan has grown impatient. His cannon have destroyed the walls in many places, but whenever he gives orders to storm the city the attackers have so far been repelled with much bloodshed. There are only two possibilities left for a military commander: either to raise the siege or, after countless attacks at single points, to order a full-scale operation to take the city by storm. Mahomet summons his pashas for a council of war, and his passionate will triumphs over all reservations. That great storm, which will finally decide matters, is to take place on 29th May. The Sultan prepares for it with his usual determination. A festival day is proclaimed; 150,000 men, from the first to the last, are to carry out all the festive customs prescribed by Islam, performing their ablutions seven times in the day, reciting the major prayers three times. All the powder and shot they have left is brought up for an intensified artillery attack to make the city ready to be stormed, and separate troops are given their positions. From morning to night, Mahomet does not allow himself an hour's rest. He rides all along the gigantic camp from the Golden Horn to the Sea of Marmara, going from tent to tent, encouraging all the leaders in person, inspiring the men. But as the good psychologist he is, he knows how to bring his 150,000 men to the highest pitch of their lust for battle, and he makes them a terrible promise, one that to his credit—or discredit—he will keep in every particular. His heralds proclaim that promise to the winds, with the sound of drums and fanfares: "Mahomet swears, by the name of Allah, by the name of Mohammed and the 4,000 prophets, he swears by the soul of his father Sultan Murad, by the heads of his children and by his sword, that after his troops have stormed the city they shall have the right to loot it as they like for three days. Everything to be found within its walls, household goods and possessions, ornaments and jewels, coins and treasure, the men, the women and the children shall belong to the victorious soldiers, and he himself will have no part in it except for the honour of having conquered this last bulwark of the eastern part of the Roman Empire."

The soldiers receive this dreadful proclamation with roars of jubilation. The loud noise of it swells like a storm, and the cry of *Allah il Allah* from thousands of voices reaches the frightened city. *Jagma, Jagma*—loot, loot! The word becomes a battle cry, with drums beating, cymbals and fanfares sounding, and by night the camp turns into a festive sea of light. Shuddering, the besieged see, from their walls, how myriads of lights and torches burn in the plain and on the hills as their enemies celebrate victory even before it is won with the sound of trumpets, pipes, drums and tambourines. It is like the cruelly loud ceremony of heathen priests before a sacrifice. But then, at midnight, all the lights are extinguished on orders from Mahomet, and the fervent roars from a thousand throats end abruptly. However, the sudden silence and the oppressive dark weigh down on the distraught listeners even more terribly than the frenetic jubilation of light and noise.

## The Last Mass in Hagia Sophia

The besieged citizens do not need anyone to make an announcement, any defector from the enemy camp, to know what lies ahead. They know that orders have been given to storm Byzantium, and presentiments of the monstrous commitment of the Turks and their own monstrous danger loom over the entire city like a storm cloud. Although it is usually split into factions of religious strife, the population gathers together in these last hours—as always, only the utmost need creates such a spectacle of earthly unity. So that they will all be aware of what they have to defend—their faith, their great past history, their common culture—the Basileus gives orders for a moving ceremony. At his command, the people all assemble, Orthodox and Catholics, clergy and laymen, children and old men, forming a procession. No one is to stay at home, no one *can* stay at home, from the richest to the poorest they gather devoutly together in that procession to sing the *Kyrie eleison* as they pass through the inner city and then go along the outer walls. The sacred icons and relics are brought from the churches to be carried at the head of the procession, and one of those holy images is hung wherever a breach has been made in the walls, in the hope that it will repel the storming of the city better than earthly weapons. At the same time Emperor Constantine gathers all the senators, the noblemen and the commanders around him, to inspire them with courage in his last speech. He cannot, however, like Mahomet promise them unlimited plunder. But he describes the honour they can win for Christianity and the whole western world if they withstand this last decisive storm, and the danger if they are conquered by those who have come to burn and murder: Mahomet and Constantine both know that this day will determine the course of history for centuries.

Then the last scene begins, one of the most moving in Europe, an unforgettable ecstasy of downfall. Those doomed to death assemble in Hagia Sophia, still the most magnificent cathedral in the world at that time, a place abandoned by the faithful ever since that day of the fraternal alliance of the two Churches. The whole court gathers round the emperor, the nobles, the Greek and Catholic priests, the Genoese and Venetian soldiers and sailors, all in armour and carrying weapons, and behind them thousands and thousands of murmuring shadows kneel in silent awe—the people of the city with their backs bowed, in a turmoil of fear and anxiety—and the candles trying to rival the darkness of the vaulting overhead light up the crowd kneeling in prayer as if it were a single body. The soul of Byzantium is praying to God here. Now the Patriarch raises his voice strongly, urging them on, and the choirs answer him. Once more the holy and eternal voice of the west answers him in the music filling this place. Then one after another they go up to the altar, the emperor first of all, to receive the consolation of the faith, until the huge cathedral is filled to high in its vaulting by a constant surge of prayer. The last Mass, the funeral Mass of the eastern Roman Empire has begun, for the Christian faith has lived for the last time in Justinian's cathedral.

After this overwhelming ceremony, the emperor returns fleetingly to his palace once more to ask all his subjects and servants forgiveness for any wrong he has ever done them in life. Then he mounts his horse and rides—like Mahomet his great enemy at the same hour—from end to end of the walls, encouraging the soldiers. It is deep night now. Not a voice rises, not a weapon clinks. Moved to their very souls, the 1,000 wait inside those walls. They are waiting for the day and for death.

### Kerkoporta, the Forgotten Door

At one in the morning, the Sultan gives the signal to attack. The great standards are unfurled, and with a single cry of *Allah, Allah il Allah* 100,000 men fall on the city walls with weapons and ladders, ropes and grappling hooks, while all the drums are beaten at the same time, all the fanfares blare and the kettledrums are struck, cymbals and flutes mingle their high notes with human cries and the thunder of the cannon into a single sound like the roar of a hurricane. Pitilessly the irregular troops, the bashi-bazouks, are flung against the walls—their half-naked bodies serving the Sultan's plan of attack to some extent, but only as buffers intended to tire and weaken the enemy before the core troops are brought into action for the final storm. Whipped on, the bashi-bazouks charge the walls in the dark, climb the battlements, storm the fortifications again and again, for they have no way of escape behind them, they are worthless human material marked out only for sacrifice. The core troops are already standing ready, driving them on to almost certain death. The defenders still have the upper hand; their coats of mail withstand the countless arrows and stones that come their way. But their real danger—and here Mahomet's calculations were correct—is weariness. Constantly fighting against the light Turkish troops pressing forward, always moving from one point of attack to another, they exhaust a large part of their strength in the manner of defence forced upon them. And now—after two hours of skirmishing day is beginning to dawn—the second line of attack, the Anatolians, are storming forward, and the battle becomes more dangerous. For the Anatolians are disciplined warriors, well trained and also wearing coats of mail; moreover, they are present in superior numbers and are well rested, while the defenders have to protect first one and then another breach against the enemy's incursions. But still the attackers are being thrown back, and the Sultan must turn to his last reserves, the janissaries, a troop of picked men, the elite guard of the Ottoman army. He places himself at the head of 12,000 young and carefully chosen soldiers, the best in Europe at this time, and with a single battle cry they fling themselves on their exhausted adversaries. It is high time for all the bells in the city to be rung to summon to the walls the last men capable of fighting, for sailors to be brought from the ships now that the crucial battle is in progress. To the undoing of the defenders, a rockfall strikes the leader of the Genoese troop, the bold condottiere Giustiniani, who is taken to the ships severely injured, and his fall makes the energy of the defenders falter for a moment. But then the emperor himself comes up to prevent the Turks breaking in, and once again the storm ladders are fended off. Determination stands against ultimate determination, and for the span of a breath it seems that Byzantium is saved, the worst of its need has withstood the wildest attack. Then a tragic incident tips the balance, one of those mysterious moments that history sometimes brings forth in accordance with its unfathomable will, and at a stroke the fate of Byzantium is decided.

Something wholly improbable has happened. A few Turks have made their way through one of the many breaches in the outer walls, not far from the real point of attack. They do not venture to attack the inner wall, but as they wander aimlessly and full of curiosity between the first and second city walls they discover that one of the smaller gates in the inner-city wall, known as the Kerkoporta, has by some incomprehensible oversight been left open. In itself it is only a small postern gate, meant for pedestrians in times of peace while the larger gates are still closed. Simply because it has no military importance, its existence has obviously been forgotten in the general turmoil of the previous night. Now, to their astonishment, the janissaries find this door in the middle of the sturdy bulwark usefully open to them. At first they suspect some trick of war, for it is so absurd that—while otherwise thousands of bodies are piled outside every breach and gap, every gate in the fortifications, while boiling oil and spears rain down—the gate here, the Kerkoporta, stands open to the heart of the city as if on a peaceful Sunday. For safety's sake they call up reinforcements, and without any resistance at all a whole troop makes its way into the inner city, suddenly attacking the unsuspecting defenders of the outer wall from behind. A few fighting men become aware of the Turks behind their own ranks, and the fatal cry rises, more murderous than any cannon in every battle, the cry of a false rumour. "The city is taken!" The Turks pass it on, louder and louder. "The city is taken!" That cry breaks all resistance. The troops of mercenaries, thinking themselves betrayed, leave their posts to get down to the harbour and the safety of the ships in time. It is useless for Constantine to fling himself and a few loyal men against the intruders; he falls unnoticed in the midst of the turmoil, and not until next day will anyone know, from the sight of crimson shoes decked with a golden eagle in a pile of bodies, that the last emperor of the eastern Roman Empire has lost his life and his empire in the honourable Roman fashion. A mote of coincidence, the forgotten door of Kerkoporta, has decided the course of the world's history.

## The Cross Falls

Sometimes history plays with numbers. The looting of Byzantium begins exactly 1,000 years after

Rome was so memorably looted by the Vandals. It is terrible to say that, true to the oath he swore, Mahomet the victor keeps his word. After the first massacre, he indiscriminately leaves houses and palaces, churches and cloisters, men, women and children to his men to be plundered, and like devils out of hell thousands of them race through the streets to get what they want ahead of someone else. The first to suffer are the churches where vessels of gold shine and jewels sparkle, and whenever the looters break into a dwelling house they hoist their banner over it, so that the next arrivals will know that the loot here has already been claimed. That loot consists not only of jewels, fabrics, money and portable goods; the women are goods for sale to seraglios, the men and children are bound for the slave market. The unfortunates who took refuge in churches are whipped out again, the old people are killed as useless mouths to feed and unsaleable ballast, the young ones, tied together like cattle, are dragged away, and along with robbery senseless destruction rages. What valuable relics and works of art the crusaders left, after indulging in what may have been an equally terrible episode of looting, are now wrecked by the victors, torn apart, valuable pictures are destroyed, wonderful statues smashed to pieces, books in which the wisdom of centuries, the immortal wealth of Greek philosophy and poetry were to be preserved for all eternity burnt or carelessly tossed aside. Mankind will never know the whole of the havoc that broke in through the open Kerkoporta in that fateful hour, or how much the intellectual world lost in the looting of Rome, Alexandria and Byzantium.

Only on the afternoon of the great victory, when the slaughtering was over, does Mahomet enter the conquered city. Proud and grave, he rides his magnificent steed past scenes of plundering without averting his gaze. He is true to his word and does not disturb the soldiers who won him this victory as they go about their dreadful business. But his way takes him first not to see what he has won, for that is everything; he rides proudly to the cathedral, the radiant head of Byzantium. For more than fifty days he has looked with longing up from his tents at the shining, unapproachable dome of Hagia Sophia; now, as the victor, he may walk through its bronze doorway. But Mahomet tames his impatience once more: first he wants to thank Allah before dedicating the church to him for all time. Humbly, the Sultan dismounts from his horse and bows his head down to the ground in prayer. Then he takes a handful of earth and scatters it on his head, to remind himself that he, too, is a mortal man who must not think too highly of his triumph. And only now, after showing his humility to God, does the Sultan rise, as the first servant of Allah to enter it, and walk into Justinian's cathedral, the church of holy wisdom, the church of Hagia Sophia.

Moved and curious, the Sultan looks at the wonderful building, the high, vaulted roof, shimmering with marble and mosaics, the delicate arches that rise from darkness into the light. This most sublime palace of prayer, he feels, belongs not to him but to his God. He immediately sends for an imam, who climbs into the pulpit and from there recites the Mohammedan confession of faith, while the Padishah, his face turned to Mecca, offers the first prayer to Allah, ruler of the worlds, heard in this Christian cathedral. Next day workmen are told to remove all signs of the earlier faith; altars are torn down, whitewash is painted over the mosaics showing sacred scenes, and the tall cross of Hagia Sophia that has spread its arms wide for 1,000 years to embrace all the sorrow in the world falls to the floor with a hollow thud.

The sound as it strikes the stone echoes through the church and far beyond, for the whole of the west shakes as it falls. The terrible news echoes on in Rome, in Genoa, in Venice; like menacing thunder it rolls to France, to Germany; and Europe, shuddering, recognizes that—thanks to its own unfeeling indifference—a fateful, destructive power has broken in through the fatal forgotten gate, the Kerkoporta, a power that will bind and cripple its own strength for centuries. But, in history as in human life, regret can never restore a lost moment, and 1,000 years will not buy back what was lost in a single hour.

# THE SEALED TRAIN

---

LENIN

---

*9 April 1917*

## The Man Who Lodges
## in the Cobbler's House

In the years 1915, 1916, 1917 and 1918 the little island of peace that is Switzerland, surrounded on all sides by the stormy tide of the World War, is the ongoing scene of an exciting detective story. The envoys of enemy powers, who only a year before used to play friendly games of bridge together and visit one another's houses, now pass in the country's luxury hotels as if they had never met before. A whole flock of inscrutable characters steal in and out of their rooms: parliamentary deputies, secretaries, attachés, businessmen, veiled or unveiled ladies, all of them on secret missions. Magnificent limousines bearing foreign emblems of distinction draw up outside the hotels, to disgorge industrialists, journalists, virtuosos and people ostensibly travelling for pleasure. But almost all of them have the same task in mind: to find something out, to act as spies. And the porters who show them to their rooms, the chambermaids who sweep the rooms, have all been urged to keep their eyes open and be on the alert. Organizations are working against each other everywhere, in restaurants, boarding houses, post offices and cafés. What is described as propaganda is half espionage, what purports to be love is betrayal, and every openly conducted business deal done by these arrivals hastily passing through has a second or third deal hidden behind it. Everything is reported, everything is under surveillance; no sooner does a German of any rank set foot in Zürich than his enemy's embassy in Berne knows it, and so does Paris an hour later. Day after day, agencies large and small send whole volumes of reports both true and fictitious to the attachés, and the attachés send them on. All the walls are transparent as glass, telephones are tapped, correspondence is reconstructed from waste-paper baskets and sheets of blotting paper, and in the end there is such pandemonium that many of those involved no longer know whether they are hunters or hunted, spies or spied on, betrayed or betrayers.

But in those days there are few reports on one man, perhaps because he is too unimportant and does not stay at the grand hotels or go to the cafés, does not attend propaganda lectures, but lives with his wife in a cobbler's house and stays out of the limelight. His lodgings are on the second floor of one of the solidly built houses in the narrow old winding Spiegelgasse, across the River Limmat, a house with an arched roof, dark with smoke partly because of time, partly because there is a little sausage factory down in its yard. His neighbours are a baker's wife, an Italian and an Austrian actor. His landlady knows little about him except that he is not very talkative, just that he is a Russian with a name that is difficult to pronounce. She deduces, from the frugal meals and well-worn clothes of the couple, whose household belongings hardly fill the little basket they brought with them when they moved in, that he left his native land many years ago and does not have much money, or a very profitable occupation.

This small, stocky man is inconspicuous, and lives in as inconspicuous a style as possible. He avoids company, and the other lodgers in the house seldom see the shrewd, dark look in the narrow slits of his eyes. He seldom has visitors. But at nine in the morning he regularly goes to the library and sits there until it closes at twelve. At ten past twelve exactly he is home again, and at ten past one he leaves the house so as to be the first reader back in the library, where he sits until six in the evening. However, as the news agencies pay attention only to those who talk a lot, they are not aware that solitary men who read and learn a great deal are always the most dangerous when it comes to instigating rebellion, so they write no news stories about the inconspicuous character who lodges at the cobbler's house. In socialist circles, he is known to have been the editor of a small radical journal for Russian émigrés, and in Petersburg as the leader of some kind of indescribable special party; but as he speaks harshly and contemptuously of the most highly regarded socialists, calling their methods erroneous, as it is difficult to get to know him, and he is not at all accommodating, no one bothers much about him. At most fifteen to twenty people, most of them young, attend the meetings that he sometimes holds in the evening in a small proletarian café, and so this loner is regarded as just one of those emigrant Russians whose feelings run high on a diet of much tea and long discussions. But no one thinks the small, stern-voiced man is of any significance, not three dozen people in Zürich consider it important to make a note of the name of Vladimir Ilyich Ulyanov who lodges in the cobbler's house. And if, at the time, one of those fine limousines racing at top speed from embassy to embassy had accidentally knocked him down in the street and killed him, the world would not know him by the name of either Ulyanov or Lenin.

*Fulfilment...*

One day—it is the 15th of March 1917—the librarian of the Zürich library has a surprise. The hands of the clock say it is nine in the morning, and the place where the most punctual of all readers in the library sits every day is empty. The clock face shows nine-thirty, then ten; the tireless reader does not come in and will never visit the library again. For on the way there a Russian friend hailed him, or rather assailed him, with the news that the revolution has broken out in Russia.

At first Lenin can't believe it. It is as if he were numbed by the news. But then he hurries off, taking short, sharp strides, to the kiosk by the banks of the lake, and he waits there and outside the editorial offices of the newspaper hour after hour, day after day. It is true. The news is true, and with every passing day, so far as he is concerned, will become, magnificently, even truer. At first it is only the rumour of a palace revolution, apparently just a change of ministers; then comes the deposition of the Tsar; the appointment of a provisional government, the Duma; freedom for Russia and an amnesty for political prisoners—everything he has dreamt of for years, everything he has been working for over the last twenty years, in a secret

113

organization, in his prison cell, in Siberia, in exile, it has all come true. All at once, it seems to him that the millions of dead demanded by this war did not die in vain. Their deaths no longer strike him as senseless, they were martyred in the cause of the new age of liberty and justice and eternal peace that is now dawning. Lenin, usually a man with such icy clarity of mind, a coldly calculating dreamer, is quite carried away by the news. And how the hundreds of others who sit in their little emigrant rooms in Geneva and Lausanne and Berne tremble, rejoicing at this happy turn of events: they can go home to Russia! Not travelling on forged passports, not entering the Tsar's realm under false names and in mortal danger, but as free citizens of a free country! They are already getting their scanty possessions ready, for the newspapers print Gorky's laconic telegram: they can all go home. They send letters and telegrams off in all directions to say they are on their way back. They must gather together, they must unite! Now they must stake their lives once again on the work to which they have dedicated themselves since their first waking hours: the Russian revolution!

## ...And Disappointment

But after a few days they are full of consternation: the Russian revolution that made their hearts rise as if on eagles' wings is not the revolution they dreamt of, is not a Russian revolution at all. It was a palace revolt against the Tsar, instigated by British and French diplomats to prevent him from making peace with Germany, not a revolution of the people calling for peace and their rights. It is not the revolution they lived for and were ready to die for, but an intrigue of the parties favouring war, the imperialists and the generals who do not want to have their plans upset. And soon Lenin and those who think like him realize that the message promising them a safe return is not for all who want the real, the radical revolution of Karl Marx. Milyukov and the other liberals have given orders not to let them in. And while the moderates, the socialists who will be useful in prolonging the war, men like Plekhanov, are helpfully conveyed back to Petersburg by Britain in torpedo boats, with an official escort, Trotsky is kept in Halifax and the other radicals outside the Russian borders. At the borders of all the states of the *entente* there are blacklists of the names of all who attended the congress of the Third International in Zimmerwald.

Lenin desperately sends telegram after telegram to Petersburg, but they are either intercepted or never delivered. What they do not know in Zürich, what almost no one knows in Europe, is very well known in Russia: how strong and energetic Vladimir Ilyich Lenin is, how purposeful and how murderously dangerous to his enemies.

The despair of those powerless radicals barred from Russia is unbounded. They have been planning their own Russian revolution for years and years, in countless General Staff meetings in London, Paris and Vienna. They have considered, assessed and discussed every detail of its organization. For decades in their journals they have weighed up against each other the theoretical and practical difficulties, dangers and opportunities. Lenin has spent his whole life considering this one complex of ideas, revising it again and again, bringing it to its final formulation. And now, because he is kept here in Switzerland, this revolution of his is to be watered down and wrecked by others, the idea of the liberation of the people, which is sacred to him, is to be put to the service of other nations and other interests. In a curious analogy, it is in those days that Lenin hears of the fate of Hindenburg in the first days of the war—Hindenburg, who has also manoeuvred and planned for his own Russian campaign, and when it breaks out has to stay at home in civilian clothing, following the progress of the generals called in and the mistakes they make on a map with little flags. Lenin, otherwise an iron-willed realist, entertains the most foolish and fantastic dreams in those days of despair. Could he not hire an aeroplane and fly to Russia over Germany or Austria? But the first man to offer his help turns out to be a spy. Lenin's ideas of flight become ever wilder and more chaotic. He writes to Sweden asking for a Swedish passport, saying he will pretend to be a mute so as not to be obliged to give information. Of course on the morning after these nights of fantasy Lenin himself always realizes that none of his crazy ideas can be carried out, but there is something else that he knows even in broad daylight—and that is that he must get back to Russia, he must put his own revolution into practice, the real and honourable revolution, not the political one. He must go back to Russia, and soon. Back at any price!

## Through Germany: Yes or No?

Switzerland lies embedded between Italy, France, Germany and Austria. The route through the Allied countries is barred to Lenin as a revolutionary; the way through Germany and Austria is barred to him as a Russian subject, belonging to an enemy power. But, absurd as it may seem, Lenin can expect a friendlier reception from Kaiser Wilhelm's Germany than from Milyukov's Russia and the France of Poincaré. On the eve of America's declaration of war, Germany needs peace with Russia at any price. So a revolutionary making difficulties there for the envoys of Britain and France can only be a welcome aid.

However, it is a great responsibility to take such a step as suddenly entering into negotiations with imperial Germany, a country that he has threatened and abused over and over again in his writings. For in the light of all previous morality it is, naturally, high treason to enter and pass through an enemy country in the middle of war, and do so with the approval of the enemy's General Staff. Of course Lenin must know that it means he is initially compromising his own party and his own cause, that he will be suspect and sent back to Russia as the hired and paid agent of the German government, and that if he realizes his programme of bringing instant peace, he will always be blamed by history for standing in the way of the real, victorious peace of Russia. And of course not only the milder revolutionaries but also most of those who think as he does are horrified when he announces his readiness, if necessary, to take this dangerous and compromising course of action. They point out in dismay that negotiations were begun long ago by the Swiss Social Democrats to bring about the return of Russian revolutionaries by the legal and neutral method of an exchange of prisoners. But Lenin knows how tedious that course of action will be, how ingeniously and intentionally the Russian government will postpone their return *ad infinitum*, while he realizes that every day and every hour counts. He sees only the aim, while the others, being less cynical and less audacious, do not dare to decide on a course of action that by all existing laws and opinions is treacherous. But Lenin has made up his own mind, and takes on himself responsibility for negotiating with the German government.

## The Pact

It is for the very reason that Lenin knows how much attention this step will arouse, and how challenging it is, that he acts as openly as possible. On his behalf, the Swiss trades union secretary Fritz Platten goes to see the German ambassador, who had already negotiated in general with the Russian emigrants, and lays Lenin's conditions before him. For, as if that insignificant, unknown fugitive could already guess at his future authority, Lenin is not asking the German government for something, but stipulating the conditions on which the travellers would be ready to accept the co-operation of the German government. The railway carriage, he insists, must have an acknowledged right to extraterritoriality. There must be no checking of passports or persons at either the start or the end of the journey. The travellers will pay for their journey themselves, at the normal rates. No one would leave the carriage either if ordered to do so or acting on their own initiative. The minister, Romberg, passes these messages on. They reach the hands of Ludendorff, who undoubtedly approves them, although there is not a word in his memoirs about what was per-haps the most important decision of his life. The ambassador tries to make changes to many details, for Lenin has intentionally phrased the document so ambiguously that not only Russians but also an Austrian like Radek could travel in the train without any inspection. Like Lenin himself, however, the German government is in a hurry—for on that day, the 5th of April, the United States of America declares war on Germany.

And thus, on 6th April at midday, Fritz Platten receives the memorable decision: "This matter approved in the desired sense." On 9th April 1917, at two-thirty, a small, poorly dressed group carrying suitcases leave the Zähringerhof Restaurant on their way to Zürich Station. There are thirty-two of them in all, including women and children. Of the men, only the names of Lenin, Sinovyev and Radek are still known. They have eaten a modest lunch together, they have all signed a document saying that they are aware of the report in the French newspaper, *Le Petit Parisien*, that the Russian provisional government intends to treat the party travelling through Germany as guilty of high treason. They have signed in clumsy, awkward handwriting, saying that they take full responsibility for this journey upon themselves and have approved all the conditions. Quiet and determined, they now prepare for their historic journey.

Their arrival at the station attracts no attention. No reporters or photographers have turned up. Who in Switzerland knows this Herr Ulyanov, the man in the crumpled hat, shabby coat and ridiculously heavy mountain shoes (he takes them as far as Sweden), in the middle of a group of men and women laden with baskets, silently and inconspicuously looking for seats in the train? They appear the same as anyone else on a walking tour: people from the Balkan states, Ruthenia and Romania often stop here in Zürich for a couple of hours' rest, sitting on their wooden cases, before going on to France and the coast, and so overseas. The Swiss Socialist Party, which has also approved of the journey, has sent no representative; only a couple of Russians have come to give the travellers a little food and messages to take to the homeland, and a few also to try to dissuade Lenin, at the last minute, from going on this "pointless, treacherous journey". But the decision has been taken. At ten past three the guard of the train gives the signal. And the train rolls away to Gottmadingen, the German border station. Ten past three, and since then the world clock has shown a different time.

## The Sealed Train

Millions of deadly shots were fired in the Great War, the weightiest, most powerful and far-reaching projectiles ever devised by ballistics engineers. But no shot went farther and was more fateful in modern history than the train that, carrying the most dangerous and determined revolutionaries of the century, races from the Swiss border across the whole of Germany to arrive in Petersburg, where it will blow the order of that time to pieces.

In Gottmadingen this unique projectile stands on the rails, a carriage of second- and third-class seats, with the women and children in second class and the men in third class. A chalk line on the floor marks off the area over which the Russians rule as a neutral zone, distinct from the compartment occupied by two German officers who are escorting this cargo of live explosive. The train rolls through the night without incident. Only in France do German soldiers, who have heard of Russian revolutionaries passing through, suddenly race up, and once an attempt made by German Social Democrats to communicate with the travellers is repelled. Lenin must know how he will expose himself to suspicion if he exchanges a single word with a German on German soil. They are welcomed ceremoniously in Sweden, and fall hungrily on the Swedish breakfast table, which serves a smorgasbord that seems to them like an improbable miracle. Then Lenin has to buy shoes to replace his heavy mountain boots, and a few clothes. At last they have reached the Russian border.

## The Projectile Takes Off

The first thing Lenin does on Russian soil is typical of him: he does not see individual people, but makes for the newspapers. He has not been in Russia for fourteen years, he has not seen the earth of his country, its flag or the uniform of its soldiers. But this iron-hard ideologist does not burst into tears like the others, does not, like the women in the party, embrace the surprised and unsuspecting soldiers. First the newspaper, *Pravda*, he wants to search it and see whether the paper, *his* paper, keeps to the international standpoint with sufficient determination. Angrily, he crumples it up. No, it does not; there is still too much about the motherland, too much patriotism, still not enough that, as he sees it, is purely revolutionary. It is time he came back, he thinks, to take the helm and impel the idea of his life towards victory or downfall. But will he get the chance? Won't Milyukov have him arrested as soon as he is in Petrograd—as the city is not yet called, but soon will be? The friends who have come to meet him are now in the train, Kamenev and Stalin, wearing strange, mysterious smiles in the dark third-class compartment, dimly lit by a light running low. They do not or will not answer his question.

But the answer given by reality is phenomenal. As the train runs into Finland Station the huge concourse is full of tens of thousands of workers, guards of honour carrying all kinds of weapons are waiting for the home-coming exile, the *Internationale* rings out. And as Vladimir Ilyich Ulyanov steps out of the train, the man who the day before yesterday was still living in the cobbler's house is seized by hundreds of hands and hoisted up on an armoured car. Floodlights are shone on him from the buildings and the fortress, and from the armoured car he makes his first speech to the people. The streets resound, and soon the "ten days that shake the world" have begun. The shot has hit its mark, destroying an empire, a world.

# WILSON'S FAILURE

———

## THE TREATY OF VERSAILLES

———

*28 June 1919*

O N 13TH DECEMBER 1918 the mighty steamer *George Washington*, with President Woodrow Wilson on board, is on its way to the European coast. Never since the beginning of the world has a single ship been awaited with so much hope and confidence by so many millions of people. The nations of Europe have been fighting each other furiously for four years; hundreds of thousands of their best young men, still in the bloom of youth, have been slaughtered on both sides with machine guns and cannon, flame-throwers and poison gas; for four years they have expressed nothing in speech or on paper but hatred and vituperation for each other. But all the bad feeling whipped up could not silence an inner voice that told them that what they said, what they did, dishonoured our present century. All these many people, consciously or unconsciously, had a secret feeling that mankind had retreated headlong into chaotic centuries of a barbarism thought to be dead and gone long ago.

Then, from the other side of the world in America, a voice spoke out clearly above battlefields still hot with blood, demanding "never war again". Never discord again, never the criminal old style of secret diplomacy that had driven nations to the slaughter without their knowledge or volition, but instead a new, better world order, "the reign of law, based upon the consent of the governed and sustained by the organized opinion of mankind". And remarkably, that voice was understood at once in all countries and all languages. The war, yesterday still a pointless quarrel about tracts of land, borders, raw materials, ore mines and oilfields, had suddenly taken on a higher, almost religious meaning: eternal peace, the messianic empire of law and humanity. All of a sudden it no longer seemed as if the blood of millions had been shed in vain: this one generation had suffered only so that such suffering would never be seen on earth again. Hundreds of thousands, millions of voices, in the grip of frenzied confidence, summoned this man; Wilson was to make peace between the victors and the defeated, and ensure that it would be a just peace. Like another Moses he, Wilson, was to bring the tablets of the new League of Nations to the peoples who had gone astray. Within a few weeks the name of Woodrow Wilson becomes a religious, a messianic power.

Streets, buildings and children are named after him. Every nation that feels in need or at a disadvantage sends delegates to him. The letters and telegrams with suggestions, requests and adjurations from all quarters of the globe arrive in their thousands and thousands, building up until whole crates of them are carried aboard the ship going to Europe. A whole part of the earth, the whole world unanimously demands this man as the arbitrator of its last quarrel before the final reconciliation of which it dreams.

And Wilson cannot defy the summons. His friends in America advise him against going to the peace conference in person. As President of the United States, they say, it is his duty not to leave his country; he would do better to conduct negotiations from a distance. But Woodrow Wilson is not to be dissuaded. Even the highest position in his country, the presidency of the United States, seems to him a small thing beside the task incumbent on him. He wants to serve not a country, not a continent, but all mankind, and not this one moment but a better future. He doesn't want to be narrow-minded and act only in the interests of America, for "interest does not bind men together, interest separates men". Rather, he wants to serve the advantage of all. He himself, he feels, must take care that military men and diplomats do not appropriate national passions again: the union of mankind would mean the death knell for their fatal professions. He must be the guarantee, in person, that "the will of the people rather than that of their leaders" is heard, and every word is to be spoken before the whole world, with doors and windows open at that congress of peace, the last, the final peace congress of mankind.

So he stands on the ship and looks at the European coast emerging from the mist, vague and formless like his own dream of the future brotherhood of nations. He stands erect, a tall man with firm features, his eyes keen and clear behind his glasses, his chin thrust forward with typically American energy, but his full, fleshy lips are closed. The son and grandson of Presbyterian pastors, he has the strength and restricted vision of those men for whom there is only one truth, and who are sure that they know what it is. He has the fervour of all his pious Scottish and Irish ancestors in his blood, and the enthusiasm of the Calvinist faith that sets a leader and teacher the task of saving sinful humanity, not to mention the obstinacy of those heretics and martyrs who would rather be burnt for their convictions than deviate one iota from the word of the Bible. And to him, as a Democrat and a scholar, the concepts of humanity, mankind, liberty, freedom and human rights are not cold words but what the gospel was to his forefathers. To him, they mean not vague, ideological concepts, but articles of religious faith, and he is determined to defend every syllable of them as his ancestors defended the message of the evangelists. He has fought many battles, but this one, he feels as he looks at the land of Europe becoming ever clearer before his eyes, will be the deciding one. Instinctively, he tenses his muscles "to fight for the new order, agreeably if we can, disagreeably if we must".

But soon the severity leaves his gaze as he looks into the distance. The cannon and flags that greet him in Brest harbour are merely honouring the president of an allied republic, but the noise he hears from the shore is, he feels, not an artificial, organized reception, not a pretence of jubilation, but the blazing enthusiasm of a whole nation. Wherever the train in which he is travelling goes, flags wave—the flames of hope—from every village, every hamlet, every house. Hands reach out to him, voices roar around him, and as he is driven into Paris down the Champs-Élysées, cascades of enthusiasm fall from the living walls. The people of Paris, the people of France, as the symbol of all the distant nations of Europe, are shouting jubilantly, they press their expectations on him. His face relaxes more and more, his teeth flash in a free, happy, almost intoxicated smile, and he waves his hat to right and left as if to greet them all and the whole world. Yes, he did right to come himself; only the vigorous will can triumph over the rigidity of the law. Can one, should one not create such a happy city and such joyfully hopeful men and women for everyone, to last for ever? One night for rest and quiet, and then he will begin the work of giving the world the peace it has dreamt of for thousands of years, thus doing the greatest deed that a human being has ever accomplished.

Journalists flock impatiently to the exterior of the palace that the French government has set aside for his use, to the corridors of the Foreign Ministry, to the Hôtel de Crillon, headquarters of the American delegation. They are an army of some size in themselves. A hundred and fifty have come from North America alone; every country, every city has sent its correspondents, and they are clamouring for tickets to let them into all the meetings. All of them! For "complete publicity" has been promised to the world. There are to be no secret meetings or agreements this time. The first of the fourteen points runs, word for word, that there shall be "open covenants of peace, openly arrived at, after which there shall be no private international understandings of any kind". The pestilence of secret agreements, which has demanded more deaths than all other epidemics, is to be defeated once and for all by the new salve of Wilson's "open diplomacy".

But, to their disappointment, the impetuosity of the journalists comes up against delaying tactics. Yes, certainly, they would all be given access to the large meetings, and the minutes of those public meetings—in reality, chemically cleaned of all causes of tension—would be conveyed to the world in full. But no information could be given yet. First the method of procedure had to be established. Disappointed, those who wanted to know more felt that there was some inconsistency here. However, they had not actually been told anything untrue. It was over the method of procedure that Wilson sensed the resistance of the Allies at the first discussion between the Big Four; they did not all want to negotiate openly, and with good reason. Secret agreements lie in the files and records of all military nations, agreements ensuring that they all get their share of the booty. There is dirty laundry that can be mentioned only in a very restricted circle. If the whole conference were not to be compromised from the first, these matters had to be discussed behind closed doors and sanitized. However, there were differences of opinion not only in the method of procedure but also at a deeper level. Fundamentally, the situation was entirely unambiguous in both groups, the American and the European, a clear opinion on the right, a clear opinion on the left. It was not just that peace was to be made at this conference; there were really two peaces to be made, two entirely different treaties. One peace was to end the war with defeated Germany, which had laid down its arms, and at the same time another, the peace of the future, was to make any future war impossible for ever. On one hand peace of the old, hard kind, on the other the new Wilsonian covenant that was to found the League of Nations. Which was to be negotiated first?

Here both points of view come up sharply against each other. Wilson takes little interest in peace only for the present day. Determining borders, paying compensation, making war reparations and so forth should, as he saw it, be left to the experts and committees on the basis of the principles established in the fourteen points. That was painstaking, detailed work, subsidiary work, work for experts on the subjects. The task of the leading statesmen of the time, on the other hand, should, and he hoped would, be what was new and coming into being, the union of nations, eternal peace. To each group, its own ideas are of pressing importance. The European Allies reasonably make the point that the exhausted and battered world cannot be left waiting months for peace to be made, or Europe will succumb to chaos. First they must get tangible matters settled, the borders, the reparations. Men still carrying arms must be sent back to their wives and children, currencies must be stabilized, trade and commerce must get going again, and only then, on an established basis, can the mirage of Wilson's project be allowed to shine brightly. Just as Wilson is not really interested in peace for its own sake, Clemenceau, Lloyd George, Sonnino, as practical men and tacticians, are really indifferent to Wilson's demands. They have paid tribute to his humane requirements and his ideas out of political calculation, and in part also out of genuine sympathy, because, whether consciously or unconsciously, they feel the captivating, compelling force of an unselfish principle on their nations; they are therefore willing to discuss his plan, qualified and watered-down to some extent. But first, however, peace with Germany as the conclusion of the war, then the covenant.

However, Wilson himself is practical enough to know how delay can affect a vital demand, leeching away its force. He himself knows how you can postpone matters by means of annoying interruptions;

no one gets to be President of the United States by idealism alone. So he inflexibly insists on his own viewpoint: the covenant must be worked out first, and he even demands its explicit verbal inclusion in the peace treaty with Germany. A second conflict crystallizes organically from this demand. As the Allies see it, building such principles into the treaty would mean granting Germany the undeserved reward of the principles of humanity in advance, after it was the guilty party that brutally infringed international law by invading Belgium, and set a terrible example of ruthlessness in General Hoffmann's negotiations at Brest-Litovsk, when Russia backed out of the Great War after the revolution. They insist on settling accounts first in the old way, in hard cash, and only then turning to the new method. Fields still lie devastated, whole cities are destroyed by gunfire. To make an impression on Wilson, the Europeans urge him to go to see them for himself. But Wilson, that "impractical man", deliberately looks past the ruins. His eyes are fixed on the future, and he sees not the cities wrecked by cannon but the everlasting construction to come. He has one task and one only: to "do away with an old order and establish a new one". Imperturbable and implacable, he persists with his demand, in spite of the protests of his own advisers Lansing and House. First the covenant. First the cause of all mankind, only then the interests of the individual nations.

It is a hard battle and it wastes a great deal of time—something that will prove disastrous. Woodrow Wilson has unfortunately omitted to define his dreams more clearly in advance. The project of the covenant that he puts forward is by no means entirely formulated, it is only a first draft, and it has to be discussed, altered, improved, reinforced or watered down at countless meetings. In addition, courtesy requires him to make visits now and then to Paris and the other capital cities of his allies. So Wilson goes to London, speaks in Manchester, visits Rome; and as the other statesmen show no enthusiasm for making progress with his project in his absence, more than a whole month has been lost before the first plenary session is held—a month during which regular and irregular troops improvise battles in Hungary and Romania, Poland and the Baltic area, occupying land, while there is a rising rate of famine in Vienna and the situation in Russia is considerably worse.

But even in this first plenary session on 18th January, it is only determined in theory that the covenant is to form "an integral part of the general treaty of peace". The document itself has not yet been drafted, it is still going from hand to hand in endless discussions. Another month goes by, a month of the most terrible unrest for Europe, which more and more clearly wants to have its real, actual peace. Not until 14th February 1919, a quarter of a year after the Armistice, can Wilson put forward the covenant in its final form, the form in which it is unanimously accepted.

Once again the world rejoices. Wilson has won his cause. In future, peace will not be kept by terror and the force of arms, but by agreement and belief in a higher law. Wilson is stormily acclaimed as he leaves the palace. Once again, for the last time, he looks with a proud, grateful smile of delight at the crowd surrounding him, sensing other nations behind this one. And behind this generation that has suffered so much he sees future generations who, thanks to this ultimate safeguard, will never again feel the scourge of war and the humiliation of dictators and dictatorships. It is the greatest day of his life, and at the same time his last happy day. For Wilson spoils his own victory by leaving the battlefield too early; and next day, 15th February, he travels back to America, to place the Magna Carta of eternal peace before his voters and countrymen, before returning to sign the other peace treaty, the last, the treaty to put an end to war.

★

Yet again the cannon thunder in salute as the *George Washington* moves away from Brest, but already the throng watching the ship leave is less dense and more indifferent. Something of the great, passionate tension, something of the messianic hope of the nations has already worn off as Wilson leaves Europe. He also meets with a cool reception in New York. No airplanes circle the ship coming home, there is no stormy, loud rejoicing, and in his own offices, in the Senate, in Congress, within his own party, the welcome is rather wary. Europe is dissatisfied, feeling that Wilson has not gone far enough. America is dissatisfied, feeling that he has gone too far. To Europe, his commitment to the reconciliation of conflicting interests in the general interest of mankind does not yet seem far-reaching enough; in America his political opponents, who already have their eyes on the next presidential election, are agitating because, they say, he has linked the new continent too closely, without justification, to the restless and unpredictable continent of Europe, thus contravening a fundamental principle of national policy, the Monroe Doctrine. Woodrow Wilson is forcefully reminded that it is not for him to found the future empire of his dreams, or think for other nations, but to keep in mind first and foremost the Americans, who elected him to represent what they themselves want. Still exhausted from the European negotiations, Wilson has to enter into new negotiations with both his own party representatives and his political opponents. Above all, he must retrospectively build a back door into the proud structure of the covenant that he thought he had constructed to be inviolable and impregnable, the dangerous "provision for the withdrawal of America from the League", allowing the United States to back out at any time they liked. That means the removal of the first stone from the structure of the League of Nations, planned to last for all eternity; the first crack in the wall has opened. It is a fatal flaw that will ultimately be responsible for its collapse.

Wilson does succeed in carrying through his new Magna Carta in America as he did in Europe, if with reservations and corrections, but it is only half a victory. He travels back to Europe, not in as free and confident a mood as he first left his country, to perform the second part of his task. Once again the ship makes for Brest, but he no longer bends the same hopeful gaze as before on the shore of France. In these few weeks he has become older and wearier because he is more disappointed, his features are sterner and tauter, a harsh and grim line begins to show around his mouth, now and then a tic runs over his left cheek, an ominous sign of the sickness gathering within him. The doctor who is travelling with him takes every opportunity to warn him to spare himself. A new and perhaps even harder battle lies ahead. He knows that it is more difficult to carry through principles than to formulate them. But he is determined not to sacrifice any part of his programme. All or nothing. Eternal peace or none at all.

There is no jubilation now when he lands, no rejoicing in the streets of Paris. The newspapers are cool as they wait to see what happens, the people are cautious and suspicious. The truth of Goethe's dictum to the effect that "Enthusiasm, unlike a pickle / Does not keep well, but may prove fickle" is felt once again. Instead of exploiting the hour while things were going well, instead of striking while the iron was hot, yielding and malleable, Wilson allowed Europe's idealistic disposition to cool off. That one month of his absence has changed everything. Lloyd George left the conference at the same time as he did. Clemenceau, injured by a pistol shot fired by a would-be assassin, has been unable to work for two months, and the backers of private interests have used those unsupervised moments to force their way into the meeting rooms of the committees. The military men have worked most energetically and are the most dangerous. All the field marshals and generals who have been in the limelight for years—whose words, whose decisions, whose arbitrary will made hundreds of thousands do as they wanted for four years—are not in the least inclined to retire into obscurity. Their very existence is threatened by a covenant depriving them of their means of power, the armies, by stating that its purpose is "to abolish conscription and all other forms of compulsory military service". So all this drivel about eternal peace, which would rob them of the point of their profession, must, at all costs, be eradicated or sidelined. They menacingly demand armament instead of Wilson's disarmament, new borders and international guarantees instead of the supra-national solution. You cannot, they say, ensure the welfare of a country with fourteen points plucked out of the air, only by providing your own army with weapons and disarming your enemies. Behind the militarists come the representatives of industrialists who keep the machinery of war running, the go-betweens who plan to do well out of reparations; while the diplomats, being threatened behind their backs by the opposition parties, and all of them wanting to acquire a good tract of land for their own countries, are increasingly hesitant. A clever touch or so on the keyboard of public opinion, and all the European newspapers, backed by their American counterparts, are playing variations in their various languages on the same theme: Wilson's fantasies are delaying peace. His Utopian ideas, they proclaim, while very praiseworthy in themselves and full of the spirit of idealism, have been standing in the way of the consolidation of Europe. No more time must be lost over moral scruples and supra-moral consideration for others! If peace is not made immediately then chaos will break out in Europe.

Unfortunately, these accusations are not entirely unjustified. Wilson, who is thinking of the centuries ahead, does not measure time by the same stand-ards as the nations of Europe. Four or five months do not seem to him much to spend on a task that aims to realize a dream thousands of years old. But meanwhile the private armies known as *Freikorps*, organized by dark powers, are marching in the east of Europe; occupied territories, large tracts of land do not yet know where they belong and which country they are to be a part of. After four months, the German and Austrian delegations still have not been received; nations are restless behind borders as yet undrawn; there are clear and ominous signs that in desperation Hungary will be handed over to the Bolshevists tomorrow and Germany the day after tomorrow. So there must be a result soon, there must be a treaty, clamour the diplomats, whether it is a just or an unjust one, and every obstacle to that treaty must be cleared away, first and foremost the unfortunate covenant!

Wilson's first hour in Paris is enough to show him that everything he built up in three months has been undermined in the single month of his absence, and now threatens to collapse. Marshal Foch has almost succeeded in getting the covenant eliminated from the peace treaty, and the work of the first three months seems to have been wasted for no good reason. But Wilson is firmly determined not to give any ground at all where the crucial points are concerned. Next day, on 15th March, he announces officially through the press that the resolution of 25th January is as valid as ever, and "that the covenant is to be an integral part of the treaty of peace". This declaration is his first measure to counter the attempt to have the treaty with Germany concluded not on the basis of the new covenant, but on the grounds of the old secret treaties between the Allied powers. President Wilson now knows exactly what those powers, who have only just solemnly sworn to respect self-determination by the nations, propose to demand. France wants the Rhineland and the Saar; Italy wants Fiume and Dalmatia; Romania,

Poland and Czechoslovakia want their own share of the booty. If he does not resist, peace will be made by the old methods of Napoleon, Talleyrand and Metternich, methods that he has denounced, and not according to the principles he has laid down and that have been solemnly accepted.

Two weeks pass in bitter dispute. Wilson himself does not want to cede the Saar to France, because he regards this first breakthrough of self-determination as setting the example for all other assumptions. And in fact Italy, feeling that all its demands are bound up with the first to be conceded, is already threatening to walk out of the conference. The French press beats its drums all the harder, Bolshevism is pushing forward from Hungary and will soon, say the Allies, overrun the world. There is ever more tangible resistance to be felt even from Wilson's closest advisers, Colonel House and Robert Lansing. Once his friends, they are now advising him to make peace quickly in view of the chaotic state of the world; rather than chaos, they say, it would be better to sacrifice a few idealistic demands. A unanimous front has closed before Wilson, and public opinion is hammering away in America behind his back, stirred up by his political enemies and rivals. There are many times when Wilson feels he has exhausted his powers. He admits to a friend that he cannot hold out much longer on his own against everyone else, and says he is determined that if he cannot get what he wants he will leave the conference.

In the midst of this battle against everyone he is finally attacked by one last enemy, the enemy within, his own body. On 3rd April, just as the conflict of brutal reality against still-unformed ideals has reached a crucial point, Wilson's legs give way under him. An attack of influenza forces him, at the age of sixty-three, to take to his bed. However, the demands of time are even more pressing than those of his fevered blood, leaving the sick man no rest. Messages of disaster flash from a gloomy sky: on 5th April Communism comes to power in Bavaria. The Munich Socialist Republic is proclaimed in that city. At any time Austria, half starving and wedged between a Bolshevik Bavaria and a Bolshevik Hungary, could join them; with every hour of resistance this one man's responsibility for everyone grows. The exhausted Wilson is pestered even at his bedside. In the next room Clemenceau, Lloyd George and Colonel House are discussing the situation. They are all determined that they must come to some conclusion at any price. And Wilson is to pay that price in the form of his demands and his ideals; his notions of "enduring peace" must, all the other statesmen unanimously say, be deferred because they block the way to a real, material, military peace.

But Wilson—tired and exhausted, undermined by sickness and the attacks of the press, blamed for delaying peace, irritated and abandoned by his own advisers, pestered by the representatives of other governments—still will not give way. He feels that he must not go against his own word, and that he will be truly fighting for peace only if he can reconcile it with the non-military and enduring peace of the future, if he tries his utmost for the "world federation" that alone will save Europe. Scarcely on his feet again, he strikes a deciding blow. On 7th April he sends a telegram to the Navy Department in Washington: "What is the earliest possible date USS *George Washington* can sail for Brest France, and what is probable earliest date of arrival Brest. President desires movements this vessel expedited." On the same day the world learns that President Wilson has ordered the ship to come to Europe.

The news is like a clap of thunder, and is immediately understood. All round the world it is known that President Wilson refuses to accept any peace that runs counter to the principles of the covenant, even if only in one point, and is determined to leave the conference rather than give way. A historic moment has come, a moment that will determine the fate of Europe, the fate of the world for decades, indeed centuries. If Wilson rises from the conference table the old world order will collapse, and chaos will ensue; but perhaps it will be one of those states of chaos from which a new star is born. Europe shivers impatiently. Will the other participants in the conference take that responsibility? Will he take it himself? It is a moment of decision.

A moment of decision. In that moment Woodrow Wilson's mind is still firmly made up. No compromise, no yielding, no "hard peace", only the "just peace". The French will not get the Saar, the Italians will not get Fiume, there will be no carving-up of Turkey, no "bartering of peoples". Right must triumph over Might, the ideal over reality, the future over the present! *Fiat iustitia, pereat mundus.* Let there be justice, though the world should perish. That brief hour will be Wilson's greatest, most humane and heroic moment; if he has the power to endure it his name will be immortalized among the small number of true friends of humanity, and he will have an unparalleled achievement to his credit. But after that hour, after that moment there will be a week in which he is assailed from all sides. The French, British and Italian press accuse him, the peace-maker, the *eirenopoieis,* of destroying the peace by theoretically theological rigidity, and sacrificing the real world to a private Utopia. Even Germany, having hoped for so much from him, and now distraught at the outbreak of Bolshevism in Bavaria, turns against him. And no less than his own countrymen Colonel House and Lansing implore him to change his mind, while his private secretary Tumulty, who had wired encouragingly from Washington a few days earlier—"Only a bold stroke by the President will save Europe and perhaps the world"—now cables from the same city, when Wilson has made that bold stroke: "…Withdrawal most unwise and fraught with dangerous possibilities here and abroad… President should… place the responsibility for a break of the Conference where it properly belongs… A withdrawal at this time would be a desertion."

Dismayed, desperate, and with his confidence disturbed by this unanimous onslaught, Wilson looks around him. There is no one at his side, they are all against him in the conference hall, all his own staff too; and the voices of the invisible millions upon millions adjuring him from a distance to stand firm and be true to himself do not reach him. He does not guess that if he carried out his threat and stood up to leave he would make his name immortal for all time, that if he did remain true to himself he would bequeath that immaculate name to the future as a postulate constantly to be invoked. He does not guess what creative force would proceed from that "No" if he announced it to the powers of greed, hatred and stupidity, he feels only that he is alone and is too weak to shoulder that ultimate responsibility. And so, fatally, Wilson gradually gives way, he relaxes his rigid stance. Colonel House acts as go-between; concessions will be made, for a week the bargaining over borders goes this way and that. At last, on 15th April—a dark day in history—Wilson agrees with a heavy heart and a troubled conscience to the military demands of Clemenceau, which have already been considerably toned down: the Saar will not be handed over for ever, only for fifteen years. This is the uncompromising Wilson's first compromise, and as if by magic the mood of the Parisian press changes overnight. The newspapers that were yesterday condemning him as the disturber of the peace, the destroyer of the world, now praise him as the wisest of all statesmen. But that praise burns like a reproach in his inmost heart. Wilson knows that he may indeed have saved peace, the peace of the present day; but enduring peace in a spirit of reconciliation, the only kind that saves us, has been lost, the opportunity wasted. Lack of sense has conquered true sense, passion has conquered reason. The world, storming a supra-temporal ideal, has been beaten back, and he, the leader and standard-bearer of that ideal, has lost the deciding battle, the battle against himself.

Did Wilson do right or wrong in that fateful hour? Who can say? At least, a decision was made, and the historic day cannot be called back. Its effects reach far ahead over decades and centuries, and we are paying the price for the decision with our blood, our despair, our powerlessness against destruction. From that day on Wilson's power, in his own time an unparalleled moral force, was broken, his prestige gone and with it his strength. A man who makes a concession can no longer stop. Compromises inevitably lead to more compromises.

Dishonesty creates dishonesty, violence engenders more violence. The peace of which Wilson dreamt as a whole entity lasting for ever remains incomplete, because it was not formed with a mind to the future or out of the spirit of humanity and the pure material of reason. A unique opportunity, perhaps the most far-reaching in history, was pitifully wasted, and the disappointed world, deprived of any element of the divine again, in a sombre and confused mood, feels the lack of it. The man who goes home, and who was once hailed as the saviour of the world, is not anyone's saviour now, only a tired, sick person who has been mortally wounded. No jubilation accompanies him, no flags are waved. As the ship sets out from the European coast, the conquered man turns away. He will not let his eyes look back at our unfortunate continent, which has been longing for peace and unity for thousands of years and has never achieved it. And once again the eternal vision of a humane world recedes into mist and into the distance.

# Also available

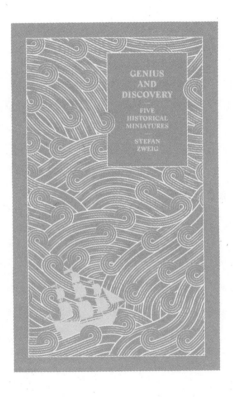

GENIUS
AND
DISCOVERY

FIVE
HISTORICAL
MINIATURES

STEFAN
ZWEIG